POETIC VOYAGES
HAMPSHIRE

Edited by Simon Harwin

with love
(pg 136)

SSadler
XXX

First published in Great Britain in 2002 by
YOUNG WRITERS
Remus House,
Coltsfoot Drive,
Peterborough, PE2 9JX
Telephone (01733) 890066

HB ISBN 0 75433 498 8
SB ISBN 0 75433 499 6

FOREWORD

Young Writers was established in 1991 with the aim to promote creative writing in children, to make reading and writing poetry fun.

This year once again, proved to be a tremendous success with over 88,000 entries received nationwide.

The Poetic Voyages competition has shown us the high standard of work and effort that children are capable of today. It is a reflection of the teaching skills in schools, the enthusiasm and creativity they have injected into their pupils shines clearly within this anthology.

The task of selecting poems was therefore a difficult one but nevertheless, an enjoyable experience. We hope you are as pleased with the final selection in *Poetic Voyages Hampshire* as we are.

CONTENTS

Cupernham Junior School

Charlie Moody	19
Meg Lawrence	20
Kristian Piper	20
Joshua White	21
Charlotte Vint	21
Lewis Packham	21
Max Hetherington	22
Jonathon Langdon	22
Alice Culliford	23
Jeremy Ferec-Dayson	23
Chealsea White	24
Ashley Medcalf	24
Sophie Lock	25
Matthew Roberts	25
Emma Anderson	26
Aaron James Medley	26
Emmaleigh Williams	27

Durlston Court School

Alex Asher	27
Chloe Harvey	28
Antonia Chope	28
Thomas Whichello	29
Hector Johnston	30
Thomas Dudley	30
Hattie Landells	31
Anna Morgan	31
Gigi Shaw	32
Nathan Solomon & Alex Vakirtzis	32
Cora Hardy	33
Emma Pritchard	34

Farleigh School

James Evans	34
Tabitha Evans	35
Patrick Henry	35
Talitha Russell	36

Rebecca Cooper	89
Louise Darley	90
James Winderam	90
Elizabeth Shearing	91
Sasha Flatau	91
Emily Underwood	92
Sophie Withers	92
Jack Murphy	93
Jack Ferrar	93
Jake Shepherd	93
Yasmin Byford	94
Luke Benford	94
Rebecca Knight	94
Iain Howarth	95
Jenny Clark	96
Natassja Shiner	97
Tom Hill	98

Oliver's Battery CP School

Francesca Benoist	98
Tom Sanders	98
Matthew Jelliffe	99

Pennington Junior School

Ella Ritchie	99
Siân Wright	99
Haydn Rickman	100
Billie Maguire	100
Marie Townsend	100
Laura Jane Rutter	101
Mikayla Warne	101
Natalie Marsh	102
Rosie Crumpton	102
Arthur Chalk	103
Andrew Jones	103
Pierce Matthews	103
Josie Lyne	104
Lee Murray	104

Stewart Humm	105
Katherine Mapes	105
Amelia Sally Hamilton	105
Robert Bailey	106
Sophie Louise House	106
Sian Bowen	107
Jordan Baker	107
Rebecca Wallis	108
Amy Broomfield	109
Lily Winslow	109
Joe Baxter	109
Abbie Brownen	110
Adam Massarella	110
Ryan James Brading	111
Katie Louise McIntyre	111
Amy Clark	111

Queens Inclosure School

Grace Spencer	112
Charlotte Pusey	112
Christopher Bond	113
Zoe Hook	114
Georgia Preston	114
Natasha Longland	115
Matthew Jenner	115
Felicity Shand	116
Curtis Murphy	116
Charlotte Roberts	116
Elena Tsibouklis	117
Sarah Hulme	117
Imogen Clarke	118
Elicia McGregor	118
Dipen Pandya	119

Romsey Junior School

Connal Dyke	119
James Perry	119
Neal Reeves	120

Wallop Primary School

The Poems

DRAGON

Its astronomical teeth glint, like a sword being drawn from its sheath,
A demon creature, its heart a volcano spewing out evil,
Its stench of putrid flesh decays the berries on the blossom,
The thrashing beast is a living nightmare that lunges at its prey,
Hovering over a geyser, boiling at a thousand degrees centigrade,
it relished the heat,
In the air a falcon, on the ground a mouse,
A prehistoric dinosaur crushing buildings like fleas,
Living in an eerie cave, it gnaws bones to the marrow.

Jonathan O'Doherty (9)

THE SEA IS AN ARMY

The sea is an army, hear its bugle sound,
Crying its plaintive cry, echoing around.
Hear the sound of people's cries, hear the horses' feet,
Hear the sound of gunshot, where the armies meet.
Crashing, rushing, hear that bugle cry,
Hear the banging of the guns, see the bullets fly.
Suddenly all is silent and still, the sea has finally won,
There is no sound of horses' feet, no banging of a gun.
Quietly now, the lapping sea is purring at the bay,
But beneath its smiling surface, you can hear it say:
'My horses lie there dormant, my bugle is un-blown,
But if the war should come again they will fight to defend their own.'

Rosemary Pritchard (11)
All Saints' CE Primary School

My Dog's Character

Food stealer
Good runner
Bad growler
Door guarder
Stranger hater
Kind hearted
Other dog snarler

My pig's character

Food taker
Huge grunter
Little grinner
Loves rolling
Hates coldness
Good sleeper
Bad eater.

Becky Savill (9)
All Saints' CE Primary School

Falling

Snow is falling to the ground,
A carpet of white can be found,
A certain chill in the winter sky,
A cloud couldn't be seen by the human eye,
People stare, they look and shout,
Specks of rain are coming out,
Night is falling very quick,
Noises can be heard, a bird, a car, a breaking stick.

Carly Craig (10)
All Saints' CE Primary School

SPRINGTIME

The warm spring sunshine on my back,
The new lambs trying to stand,
The farmer taking seeds from the sack,
Planting on the dry land,
The field filled with daisies fills me with joy
As I pick them one by one,
I wish this joy would never end.

Kerri Chadwick (10)
All Saints' CE Primary School

NETBALL

N etball players warming up
E verybody's watching
T eam players wish to win the cup
B all is falling in the air
A unties, uncles cheering them on
L onging to get the ball
L aughing in embarrassment.

Kirsty Petch (9)
All Saints' CE Primary School

STING!

S tyled in black.
T empting the moonlight he says
I have the blackest heart and
N othing can stop me from conquering the business
G azing to the floor he knows wrestling will only lead to
   a deadly human torch match.

Stephen Nock (11)
All Saints' CE Primary School

WATERLOO

As we marched through the river
On the cold, damp morning,
We were frightened,
But excited,
We heard victory calling.

As we saw our brave men killed
And young boys scream in terror,
We felt powerless
And defeated,
Till we realised Boney's error.

As we gazed on the battlefield,
The brave Scots Greys were charging,
They were fearless,
Ambushed, slaughtered,
As the Lancers came from hiding.

As we heard the Prussians singing,
We knew the war was ended,
Some were laughing,
Others crying,
Wounds needing to be mended.

Simon Boult (10)
All Saints' CE Primary School

THE GREAT TRAIN ROBBERY

Here is a boy called Donald McBrain,
Who came to the station to catch the train,
But saw the post-train running away,
As if it were going on its holiday.

Then here came help in the form of two guards,
Who hauled the boy on, whilst singing ballads
And made him most comfy in their little van,
For McBrain was exhausted, because he had ran.

The train gave a judder and then a small jolt,
For a bad crook had loosened a catch and a bolt.
The crook (whose name was Mr Macosh)
Was robbing the train of a huge load of dosh.

Now Donald, who had the most sensitive ears,
Had heard a bit more than a few of his peers.
He heard the crook's footsteps, all over the train
And then was quite worried, poor Donald McBrain.

McBrain warned the guards, who then got to their feet,
They then walked down the train and the thief they did meet.
The crook was then caught and put in a cop's van
And the post-train was saved from the devious plan.

David Hughes (10)
All Saints' CE Primary School

FOOTBALL

F oul player: yellow card
'O ff the pitch,' the referee said
O n the bench and rest your head
'T hat's not fair,
B ecause he was fouled.'
A lmost a great goal
L oving fans, cheering them on
L aughing at you because you lost.

Liam McHugo (11)
All Saints' CE Primary School

RIVERS

Peaceful rivers slowly flow
Over sleeping brooks
Animals and birds
Silent sleeping
Under the starry moonlit sky

The swaying trees
Were like golden curtains,
Dancing in the summer breeze,
The forest noises were like
A musical band accompanied
By the rustling leaves

As the glowing sun rose up
Like a ball of fire
Animals arouse to meet the day
And began to stir
The world was awake again.

Kerry Wilkes (11)
Ashley Junior School

MIDNIGHT PEACE

Twinkling stars sleeping silently in the moonlit sky,
Soft silver rivers flows happily,
The moon was like a shiny ball of glitter,
Midnight blue sky was a sea of peace.

Massive green trees sway helplessly,
Small bunny rabbits hop merrily,
The calm wind would blow softly not to disturb sleep and to
Give children sweet dreams.

As the sun went down the magnificent moon came up,
Everyone begins calm sleep,
When the stars appear everything turns to silver,
As the sun drifts up the moon falls down and day is here again.

Lorna Heaton (10)
Ashley Junior School

THE VERY GORY TRUTH ABOUT NIGHT!

Night is scary with murdering ghosts and flesh eating ghouls
Bloodsucking bats which fly around schools
Veins slurping trees attack with no warning
Death is near don't come out until morning!

Rats with rabies threaten to bite
So don't come out without a light
Enormous bears stand up tall
Like man eating vultures devouring a blood ball!

Bottomless pits filled with dead bodies
Coming to life turning into zombies
All this mixed is not well
It is like a living hell!

Kane Ciaputa (11)
Ashley Junior School

PITCH-BLACK AND NOWHERE TO GO

Inky shadows creeping along dark alleys
Gruesome monsters ambushing their dinner
Huge, gloomy graveyards waking up
Witches roaming the noir black sky
Everything's waiting, waiting, waiting.

Everything is waiting for a wrong move
Storms are brewing and breaking free
Dark magic's woven above the stars
Nightmares creeping into your mind.

Wrinkled trees look like zombies
Crooked houses look like giants
Transfixing head lamps look like UFOs
Lurking humans look like kidnappers
Everything's waiting, waiting, waiting.

Everything's waiting for a wrong move
Storms are brewing, breaking free
Dark magic's woven above the stars
Nightmares creeping into your mind.

Lauren Szumski (11)
Ashley Junior School

PANTHER

The panther is a dark black cloud,
Eyes like streaking white lightning,
A roar like booming thunder,
She slips through the shadows unnoticed.

The panther is a dark black cloud,
She is a creature of the night,
She watches her prey,
Rolling her black tongue over her gleaming white teeth.

The panther is a dark black cloud,
She is sleek and elegant,
Her soft fur is velvety and pitch black
And her padded paws are silent as she prowls through the night.

The panther is a dark black cloud,
She glides across the damp grassy jungle floor,
Her glossy razor sharp claws,
Emerge from her paws and she is ready to kill.

Poppy Sharp (10)
Ashley Junior School

MY MAGIC CUPBOARD

I will put in the cupboard
A flake of glistening snow
A clap of roaring thunder
A bolt of cracking lightning

I will put in the cupboard
A planet of fun and games
The feeling of dreadful hate
The sound of colour

I will put in the cupboard
A horse on a farm
A rat hungry for warmth
A farmer planting money trees

My cupboard is made from seashells
and old wrecked ships
The door is made of an untold story
In my cupboard I can time travel to
places that have never been found
and read the stories that can never be read.

Jamie Mitchener (10)
Ashley Junior School

RIVER FLOWING SLOWLY

Silver stars sleeping silently like a baby in his cot
Golden moon drifting peacefully in the dark night sky
River flowing slowly
Like the wind rustling the branches

Silent trees swaying swiftly in the dark, peaceful forests
Floating clouds drifting quietly like fluffy pink candyfloss at the fair
River flowing slowly
As sparkling fish drift along

Muddy field waiting sadly like a lonely child
Darkening nights turning slowly from dark to light
Like lights being switched on and off
River flowing slowly
Reflecting pale yellow moon across the starry sky.

Kurt Britton (11)
Ashley Junior School

NIGHT

Night comes,
The moon breaks through the clouds,
Small creatures creep out of their nests
And the gloomy dark shadow mysteriously
Haunts the deserted and atmospheric streets.
Bats fly around the graveyard,
Looking for a midnight feast.
The ghostly owl swoops like a spirit of night as
It soars through the glimmering night sky.
Figures move camouflaged in the bush waiting for
The perfect moment to creep into the house.
The night finally turns to morning.

Sam Graham (10)
Ashley Junior School

STARLESS AND BIBLE-BLACK

Hell like ghosts prowling around the dark, gloomy churchyard
The silver moon sailing in the starless and bible black sky
Shadows cast over forest plains leaving only blackness
Making the day die.

In the forest, faces show, upon the woodland trees
Then all the forest animals feel a cold, steady breeze
The people of the forest sleep calm and carelessly
But the bats are still bloodsucking to set some blood free.

But here I am safe in my bed
Resting my tired, sleepy head
But what's that I see over there
Prowling around the bottom stair?

Nick Hedger (11)
Ashley Junior School

THE RIVER

Trickling, glistening and moonlit silver
Below the stunning stars.
Although in the day fierce and frightening
        At night silent and calm.

Its glowing azure colour
Is unintimidating in every way
The moon provides a ribbon of light
Under the starry sky.

Its silky ripples, tranquil and calm,
Its beauty beams out far.
Reflecting, glittering, twinkling stars
Meandering on its way.

Lizzie Curtis (11)
Ashley Junior School

MY MAGIC BOX

I shall put in my box
The teddy that takes twenty cuddles a day,
The fun of finding a letter full of comforting words,
The fantastic appetising smell of pizza coming up the stairs.

I shall put in my box
The computer that sits in my mind,
The memories that sit in my room,
The fright of going on a scary fair ride.

I will put in my box
The enjoyment of eating chocolate ice cream,
The softness of a hamster,
The shock of a goose biting your finger.

I will put in my box
The laugh of looking back on being chased by a tiny dog,
The excitement of waking up on Christmas Day,
The look of a sweet, little monkey.

I shall make my box with a chocolate lid
A toffee handle and a caramel base.

In my box I shall bungee jump off Mount Everest
and land in a pile of jelly.

Martin Price (9)
Ashley Junior School

THE MAGIC BOX

In the box I shall put
    A huge, white mountain covered in fluffy snow
    Happy memories of jolly times.

In the box I shall put
    The squawking of a giant vulture
    flying over the African plains.

In the box I shall put
    A frozen over pond that changes colour
    every time you look at it.

In my box I shall put
    The voices of my best friends
    to keep me company when I feel lonely.

In the box I shall put
    A rainforest full of tropical animals
    that sing and play all the time.

My box is made from white chocolate
fresh from out the wrapping.
It has a black key to keep it safe.

In my box I can snowboard on the new, white snow
or I can talk to all my friends.

Katie Morris (10)
Ashley Junior School

THE MAGIC BOX

I will put in my box
The purr of my pussy cat playing,
A hug from my mum in the morning,
The fun with my favourite friends.

I will put in my box
My dad in a tennis court,
Tim Henman at home,
The last joke I was told.

I will put in my box
The memory of my mum,
My cat doing history,
Me at home.

I will put in my box
The racket of Tim Henman,
The silver snake slithering slowly,
The last race I ran.

My box is made from clouds, gold and water,
With tennis balls in the corner and clothes on top,
A skeleton jaw for a hinge.

I shall snowboard in my box
On the white cream snow,
And slide like a bird in flight.

Sebastian Bartlett (9)
Ashley Junior School

THE MAGIC BOX

In my box will go
    a beam from the sun,
    a gust from the wind,
    a drop from the sky.

In my box will go
    the sound of a smooth snake slithering,
    the soft trotting of a horse,
    the brilliant blow of a basking bear.

In my box will go
    the loud honk of a car,
    the speed of a racing fan,
    the soft whoosh of a motorbike.

In my box will go
    the sticky suckers of an octopus,
    the sharp teeth of a shark,
    the angler's fishing light.

My box is made from the hard core of a diamond
with the secrets of the earth on the sides,
then the jaws of a viper for hinges
and the skull of a monkey for a lock.

I can change shape in my box
with snow that is warm and dry
and everything is immortal.

Samuel Brook (9)
Ashley Junior School

THE MAGIC BOX

I will put in my box
A giggle from a girl,
A happy heart,
A smiling family.

I will put in my box
A friendly friend,
The tick-tock of the clock,
A whizzing world.

I will put in my box
The first smile from my sister,
My mum and dad as happy as can be,
A happy country.

I will put in my box
A drop of the sun,
A shine of the rain.

My box is made from a swift of the whitest cloud,
The secrets are hidden in the blue air
And the hinges are made from the lightest droplets of rain.

In my box I will go for a calm, smooth ride in the clouds
And meet loads of famous people,
Then swiftly fall down into my bed.

Georgia Miller (10)
Ashley Junior School

THE MAGIC BOX

I will place in my box
the sting of a stinging nettle
the whistle of the wind whistling in the trees
the shine of the sun.

I will put in my box
the rage of a dragon
the poison of a snake
the growl of a bear.

I will put in my box
the splash of water sloshing in the sea
the speed of a shark
the shock of an eel.

My box is made from
the slime of a slug
with rubies on the lid
and skulls in the corners
its hinges are sharks' teeth.

I can travel in my box
I could go snowboarding
I could fly or drive around in my box
and I could sail the Seven Seas.

Joe McIntosh (9)
Ashley Junior School

THE MAGIC BOX

I will put in the box
The purr of my pussy cat as he lays on my pillow
The playing of my pretty little puppy
The comforting hug of my mum.

I will put in the box
The kind kiss of my dad
The greeting of my pets
The smile of my friends.

I will put in the box
The smirky grin of my brother
The chatter of my cousin
My caring family.

I will put in the box
The trot of my horses
My puppy plodding down the road
My horse stealing all of my stuff.

My box is made from rubies and diamonds
The softness of a baby's skin and shining silk
The hidden secrets of history
And all the colours of the rainbow.

I shall travel round the world in my box
Catch the goldness of the sun
I will find the end of a rainbow
And float on a cloud.

Francesca Ware (10)
Ashley Junior School

THE NIGHT

As night turns,
The soft darkness,
Surrounds the world
In its gentle, velvet arms.

As the road quietens down,
The street lights shine
The light of the world
As people sleep peacefully.

The refreshing wind
Blowing softly,
Is the breeze of the
Coming new day.

Tom Hynd (10)
Ashley Junior School

ART

The clay we use is white
The sky we draw is blue
If I felt clever enough
I would draw a picture of you.

I tried to draw a car
But it didn't turn out quite right
Because when I coloured it in
It looked more like a bike.

So I went to see the teacher
To ask her what to do
She said if I didn't practise every day
I would be as bad as you.

Charlie Moody (7)
Cupernham Junior School

LATE FOR SCHOOL

In comes Mum, late again,
'Hurry up children,' she squawks like a hen.
'Chew up your breakfast, Mary!
Do your teeth Carey!
Five minutes to leave the house
'Mary, stop eating like a mouse!
Mary, tie your shoes laces.
Oh! look at your dirty faces!'
Out of the house quick, quick, quick.
'Mum, the dog's been sick!'
'Just leave the house, run, run, run.'
'Mum, going to school's not much fun!'
At school at last,
Oh blast!
It's the weekend.

Meg Lawrence (8)
Cupernham Junior School

HUNTING FOR BONES AND FOSSILS

Hunting, hunting bone, hunting fossil
Hunt dinosaur bones, animal bones
Human bones that have broken.

Hunting, hunting bone, hunting fossil
Hunt leaf fossils, insect fossils,
Helix fossils, all dusty and golden.

Kristian Piper (7)
Cupernham Junior School

I LOVE TO GO TO LUNCH

I love to go to lunch
It's my favourite time to munch
I eat all my food
And try not to be rude
And make sure I don't give anyone a punch.

Joshua White (8)
Cupernham Junior School

SNOW ON CHRISTMAS DAY

Sisters in the snow sharing secrets
That they already know
Little children standing in the cold
Thinking that they are going to catch a cold
Snowflakes on noses and red, rosy cheeks
Leaves on the ground everywhere around
Fields covered in blankets of snow
We leave footprints wherever we go.

Charlotte Vint (8)
Cupernham Junior School

SPRING

Leaping sheep and mooing cows
Singing birds tweeting to each other
And leaves spreading out
Sun shining overhead
Flowers blooming big and bright.

Lewis Packham (7)
Cupernham Junior School

MY TEACHER IS AN ALIEN!

My teacher is an alien
She's tall and thin and green
She flies to school in a UFO
It's the strangest thing you've seen!

My teacher scares the pupils
They're quivering with fear
I don't know why they're frightened -
I think it's her sixth ear!

My teacher's never boring
And her lessons are quite fun
I'm sure she's the only teacher
Who's flown around the sun!

Max Hetherington (7)
Cupernham Junior School

ROUGH PLAYING IN MY BEDROOM

Toys are all over the floor
Screwed up duvet
Drinks spilt all over the floor
Bits of a biscuit are on the floor too
Bears and cuddly toys all over the floor and bed
Windows broken glass all over the window sill
My friends are fighting under the bed
Shouting at each other and being silly
Smashed lights
Mum comes in 'Oh no, Jonathon!'
'Sorry Mum.'

Jonathon Langdon (8)
Cupernham Junior School

SUMMER HOLIDAY

Friday, it's the end of term,
Yippee, hooray, no more school,
Time to run and see your friends,
Yes, the holidays are cool!

Jumping, skipping, hopping, running,
All of us we love to play,
In the park we swing and slide,
My friends and I, through the day.

I love going to the beach,
Where I can have some fun,
I am going to eat ice cream
And sunbathe in the sun.

I like the summer holidays,
Each day there's loads to do,
Although at school there's lots of work,
I really love it too!

Alice Culliford (8)
Cupernham Junior School

THE LITTLE OWL

The little owl flew out one night
giving the little mice a very big fright.
She makes a shadow against the moon,
her call sounds like 'Seee youuu sooon.'
Then she dives into her hollow,
to get the little vole she will swallow.

Jeremy Ferec-Dayson (7)
Cupernham Junior School

SOMEBODY'S COMING ROUND TODAY

Somebody's coming round today
Somebody's coming to play
Jessica's coming round today
Hip hip hooray
We will have lots of fun
Playing in the garden in the sun
If we are good Mummy might take us to the park
Where we can play on the swings and slides until it gets dark
Then we will go to Captain Banana's for our tea
For chicken nuggets, chips and peas
Then home for a bath
We've had a good laugh
Time for bed
Two sleepy heads.

Chelsea White (7)
Cupernham Junior School

SNOWING PLAYTIME

Children sliding on slippery slides
Children skating on icy paths
Children slipping on slippery patches
Children scooping up snowballs
Children skidding along the path
Children shivering in the cold
Children skiing down ramps
Children sledging down hills
Children spinning on the ice
Children shouting in the snow
Children shovelling the snow
Children watching the sun melt the snow.

Ashley Medcalf (7)
Cupernham Junior School

CHRISTMAS MORNING

People walking down the street,
With their winter frozen feet.

Children jumping in the snow,
With the wind a howling blow.

The roof is glistening in the air,
What is that I can hear?

Can you hear the trees swaying,
Or the little children playing.

What is it that you can hear?
I can hear the Christmas deer.

Sophie Lock (8)
Cupernham Junior School

ICY PLAYTIME

Slipping and sliding
Slipping and sliding
All over the place
They're all trying hard
Not to fall over
Onto the concrete floor.

Slipping and sliding
Slipping and sliding
All over the place
They're thinking 'Be sensible'
Well, I think they should
They're spilling their food all over the door.

Matthew Roberts (8)
Cupernham Junior School

COMING HOME ON A SUMMER'S EVENING

I'm walking home
I can't wait until I can have a water fight
Home at last
Chasing in and out of the swing
'Oh no, I've run out of water'
Quick, through the back door
Oh no, Mum is standing in the doorway
'Something wrong Mum?'
'Bath time for you'
'Oh, but Mum!'
'OK, 30 minutes more'
He's waiting behind the wall
He's got me
Game's over!

Emma Anderson (8)
Cupernham Junior School

A FROSTY PLAYTIME

Skidding on the ice
And it is very nice
Playing in the snow
Where the wind can blow
Getting snowballs
When the snow falls
Playing ice hockey
With a doggy
Hats and scarves
To keep warm
A bucket and spade
Full of snow.

Aaron James Medley (7)
Cupernham Junior School

THE WET PLAYTIME

We're out to play
But the sky turns grey
The rain starts falling
The teacher starts calling
Get off the grass
Go into your class
The weather's not fine
So it's a wet playtime

The rain starts pouring
Get inside for some drawing
Talk to your friends
Until playtime ends
No more messing
It's time for lessons
That was a wet playtime.

Emmaleigh Williams (7)
Cupernham Junior School

THE NIGHT OF FIRE-STARS

The sky is filled with flashing firelights,
The whoosh, the crackle, a magical sight,
The whiz, the scream, the colours so bright,
The zip, the zoom, like a bird in flight,
They creep, they slither, they do not dither,
The sparks fly high like shards of glass,
They are just like a blizzard about to pass,
They fling off flames the colour of Mars,
That's what it's like on the night of fire-stars.

Alex Asher (10)
Durlston Court School

THE LADY IN THE LAKE

The Lady in the Lake
Makes no sound
The Lady in the Lake
Hears all around

The Lady in the Lake
Is all so white
The Lady in the Lake
Is all so bright

The Lady in the Lake
Is just so cold
The Lady in the Lake
Is not to be told
That Merlin the Master
Is just so magic
The Lady in the Lake
Is not that tragic

The Lady in the Lake
Is just so cold
The Lady in the Lake
Is not to be told.

Chloe Harvey (10)
Durlston Court School

MY DOG

My dog is black and brown,
He runs around and round,
Chasing bones and catching balls,
His tail is never found.

I love my dog,
When he's not in a bog,
Forever muddy, yet still so cuddly,
He'll always be my best dog.

Antonia Chope (10)
Durlston Court School

THE LITTER BOY

Henry Williams, you ungrateful boy!
Littering that empty sweet packet
That crumbling, crisping crisp packet
That all should be in the bin
And are they even allowed in school?

How many times do I have to tell you?
Just throwing around that paper ball
For no reason except it litters the floor
And is that *your* rotting apple core?

How many times do I have to tell you?
You dreadful little demon boy
Pick up all that rubbish
Just falling out of your pocket.

How many times do I have to tell you?
It's been three years you've been littering now
And now the world is covered
With sweet wrappers and candy bars
I can't even see you now
So I will tell you once more
Don't litter on the floor!

Thomas Whichello (9)
Durlston Court School

WAR

War is nasty,
War is cruel,
War is just an enormous duel.

War can cause such suffering,
War can cause such pain,
But in the end there's nought to gain.

War is pointless,
War is fruitless,
War is just a bloody mess.

War can cause destruction,
War can cause damage,
But in the end it's all so savage.

War causes death,
War causes crime,
But in the end it can never rhyme.

Hector Johnston (10)
Durlston Court School

ANIMAL ANTICS

Bats are sleeping
    While
Cats are peeping
    On their prey
    While
Cheetahs are running
Lions are cunning
    Every
    Day.

Thomas Dudley (11)
Durlston Court School

LIFE

Life is like a roller coaster
Looping up and down
With very strange happenings
Whizzing all around.

Life is like a clock
Going clang, clang, clang
But if you're not careful
It might just go bang.

Life is like the TV
Changing channels all the time
On number 3 it's ITV
A good mood all the time.

Hattie Landells (10)
Durlston Court School

THE SEA

I went to see the sea,
The sea I went to see
And swimming in the sea,
I saw silly Sam.

Silly Sam was swimming,
swimming in the sea,
Silly Sam saw me,
Slapping in the sea.

He saw a silly shark,
Swimming in the sea,
'Snap!' goes the silly shark,
Sam ate me.

Anna Morgan (11)
Durlston Court School

THE SUN AND MOON

Crimson, shining,
Eternal light,
A sphere of flame,
Oh so bright!

Golden brilliance,
An orange in the sky,
A symbol of hope,
Oh so high!

Silver, snowy,
Like death itself,
Shimmering hauntedly,
Oh rising with such stealth!

Luminous potion on a mad man's shelf,
Flickering rainbow colours, diamond bright,
A nocturnal sun,
Oh such a sight!

Gigi Shaw (10)
Durlston Court School

STRESS

Stress, stress, stress
All day long
My head screams bong, bong, bong
It's madness!

Stress, stress, stress
When will it stop?
I'm afraid my brain might pop
When will I ever rest?

Stress, stress, stress
Makes me cry to death
Must take a breath
Will it bring me illness?

Stress, stress, stress
I always get shouted at
By some old bat
Please give me less!

Nathan Solomon & Alex Vakirtzis (10)
Durlston Court School

SNOW

Crisp and white in the night,
Flowing, blowing, glowing bright,
Cold as ice, swift as sleet,
Revolving round like a fleet.

Hiding tunnels, covering ground,
Ever going round and round.
Sending shivers down my spine,
Hardly taking any time.

Sharp as wasps, cold as death,
Very like old Macbeth,
Now as day dawns,
The sun's gold adorns.

The snow must go,
No more to blow,
Crisp and white in the night,
Flowing, blowing, glowing bright.

Cora Hardy (11)
Durlston Court School

THE CONCENTRATION CAMP

I'm captured in a concentration camp,
There's no life there, just a musty lamp.
I feel like a bowl of rotten stew,
The smell is horrible, phew!
The death is increasing more and more,
The screams are like a lion's roar.
Children and grown-ups death awaits,
No food at all, just terrifying fates.
I wish I wasn't here, it's the worst of all,
Life is a death trail, no fun at all.
I pray all the time, hoping for freedom,
Nothing is new though, just deteriorating scum.
I wish I could leave but I know I can't,
Hearing the soldiers piercing rant.
This is the worst of all the lairs,
A concentration camp is an horrific nightmare.

Emma Pritchard (10)
Durlston Court School

THE BLACK NIGHT

Outside an abandoned house,
Cats miaow and a fox creeps
Along the grass,

Silence!

Then small crunchy sounds
All around,
As you walk across the
Frosty grass,
Somewhere an owl is hooting.

James Evans (9)
Farleigh School

FIERY DEATH

Something in the darkness
Lurching side to side
Suddenly all around is brightness
Suddenly he died

Fiery breath
Guarding treasure
Fiery death
For ever and ever

Teeth like those of shark
Claws like shimmering silver
Then once more it's dark
It waits . . .
. . . for you!

Tabitha Evans (10)
Farleigh School

THE NIGHTMARE HOUSE

Creaking floorboards,
Tapping at the window,
Wallpaper ripping,
Turning, screaming, running,
Scratching noises fill the air,
Nerves tightening,
Owls hooting,
Footsteps on the floorboards,
Moonlight floods the room,
Leaves crunching,
Footsteps approaching!

Patrick Henry (8)
Farleigh School

FLOWERS

Flowers are pretty
Flowers are sweet
People who are witty
Like gardeners go to sleep.

We lovingly plant them from the seeds
Then spend the summer freeing from weeds
Better a daisy chain than beads
How well the fairies know our needs.

When flowers are wide awake
They nod their heads and quake
When humans dare to take
Them from the wild
We should think for flowers' sake
To leave them in their place, not take.

The flowers are tired, they droop their heads
They've gone to sleep in their beds
Some are alive, some are dead
We'll find out in the spring ahead.

Talitha Russell (10)
Farleigh School

THE NOISES OF THE NIGHT

Squeaking bats flying around,
Wind blowing, whooshing
Through the trees,
Twigs snapping,
Owls screeching as they hunt
For their prey.

Edward Eley (8)
Farleigh School

A WARM WINTER

It's cold outside
The wind is blowing,
But we're inside
Where the fire's glowing.

Whilst we hang up mistletoe
Green ivy and holly,
We look out at the snow
And feel warm and jolly.

The lights on the tree glisten,
Our stockings hang empty on the bed,
And later we will listen
For Santa on his sled.

We leave carrots and a mince pie,
And say we will not peep.
I snuggle up as I lie
And finally fall asleep.

Lydia Bluring (10)
Farleigh School

MY NIGHT POEM

The frozen grass glistens
   In the dark starry night,
A blurry shadow of a deer
   Nibbling the grass.

The wind is strong blowing
   Through the trees,
Smell the smoky scent in the air,
   As the world sleeps till dawn.

Gennie Allcott (8)
Farleigh School

PETS

Pets, pets,
Little and furry,
Huge and rough,
Long and slimy.

Cats are scratching at big, brown doors,
Dogs are barking at strange-looking people,
Rabbits are nibbling at fresh, green salad.

Hamsters are sleeping in sawdust and bedding,
Guinea pigs are eating juicy, red lettuce,
Fish are swimming in clear fish tanks.

Tortoises are crawling in grass and twigs,
Lizards are climbing on long, tall branches,
Snakes are slithering in hedges and trees.

Pets, pets,
Always eating,
Always busy,
Always fun!

Harriet Jackson (8)
Farleigh School

A HAUNTED HOUSE

In the house there's black stillness,
Hairy spiders are crawling all around,
Hideous bats and screeching rats.

Outside owls are hooting,
Cunning foxes moving about,
Timid cats are catching prey.

Melissa Vernon (8)
Farleigh School

SPACE TRAVEL

Space travel is a wonderful thought,
It makes things go pop on the countdown to nought.
You zoom through the air,
Like a fox or a hare.
You whirl round and round,
Like a circus clown.

You see planets and stars,
Like Jupiter and Mars.
There are galaxies and black holes,
Solar systems and worm holes.
There are laser guns and battlefields,
Spaceships and force fields.

Space travel is definitely a wonderful thing.

Stephen Cooke (10)
Farleigh School

MY DOG, JOSEPH

I waited a long time
For my wish to come true
I've got my own dog now
And he's Joseph - that's who.
He drives Mamma mad
Cos he eats from the bin
He's furry and sweet
And he's not very thin.
When you throw a ball
He runs and he pounces
But when he gets it
The ball just bounces.

Arthur Guinness (9)
Farleigh School

ONE SNOWY DAY

One snowy day,
Some children went out to play.
Trees covered in frost,
People getting lost,
White all around,
People jumping up and down.

A snowman they built,
All flat and on a tilt,
Then tobogganing down the lane,
People waved, laughed and played,
Red cheeks aglow,
People loving all the snow.

They stayed out long,
While the sun was in the sky,
The frost and the snow,
Melting all the while,
Skating, skiing, sleighing,
Winter can be so much fun.

Talana Adams (10)
Farleigh School

I LOVE SPRING

I love spring,
It's the best time of year,
Sun shining,
Daffodil blooming, trees blossoming.
Sheep, goats, cows, ducks, horses
Are having their young.
But the best thing of all is it's my birthday.

Toby Wicks (9)
Farleigh School

MY SISTER

I have a sister called Suzannah
She really is a pain
If I had the option
I'd flush her down the drain
She is a brilliant swimmer
She really goes quite fast
I wish that I could swim like that
Because she goes flying past
She really is a bossy boot
She orders me around
She tells me to find something
And won't stop until it's found
She really can be nice sometimes
She is a super sis
If ever she should go away
I would really be amiss.

James Pope (10)
Farleigh School

MY HAMSTER

I've got a new hamster
He is called Fudge
He is very jumpy
But he is very lovely
He is a big baby
He is very sweet
He is a great thing to have at school
He keeps me company.

Camilla Wright (10)
Farleigh School

PARADISE LAND

My paradise land is far away,
I have often dreamed of going there.
Tall trees blow in the wind over warm beaches,
A deep blue sea has multicoloured fish swimming in gentle waves,
The peace is disturbed by the sound of neighing horses,
They charge through the surf,
Their manes and tails catching the light
And all at once they disappear.
I look around and notice far on the horizon a field of flowers,
Golden puppies are tumbling by their mothers,
I want to join them so I start to walk slowly,
But my fantasy fades in front of me,
Until I dream again.

Alison McDonagh (9)
Farleigh School

A POEM OF SWEETIES

Sweeties are yummy,
Sweeties are scrummy,
Some sweets are small,
Some sweets are cool.

I like eating sweeties,
Big ones and small.
Gobstoppers, marshmallows,
I like them all.

If you like all sweeties,
As much as I do,
Then come to the shop,
Where they've got some for you.

Sophie White (9)
Farleigh School

THE OWL

Tap, tap, tap
There was an egg and it hatched
A head popped out
Followed by a body
Tiny squeaks waiting to be fed
It grew and grew
It left the nest for the first time
It flew and glided, then flapped its wings
It swooped and rose and dived and hovered
During the day it slept
By night it soared down
And snatched its prey
Furry, small and running
The end of a life
It met another owl
And a new life started again.

Joel Hulmes (9)
Farleigh School

ANIMALS

Big or small, strong or weak
They sound amazing, you have to admit
Some are dangerous, some are not
I would like to tell you about these things

Some will dig, some will not
They live on sea and land but you can see them everywhere
Each one has a beautiful colour
Some are striped, some are spotted and some are plain
Some have scales or fur
These wonderful things are *animals.*

Barnaby Hunter (9)
Farleigh School

NIGHT FEELINGS

I lie in bed, it's a long night,
I wonder,
My mind thinking of watching people.

I begin to count sheep,
No use,
Time wanders on as the
Witching hour aproaches
    Fast!

Floorboards creak,
Owls hoot,
Foxes kill,
I just lie in bed,
I can't stop thinking.

Matthew Guinness (8)
Farleigh School

SUMMER DAYS

On summer days
When the sun is up in the clear blue sky
The poppies open with their flaming red petals
Gentle breezes blow the golden corn
And the lambs prance on the fresh green grass.

Happy children play in the glistening sea
They build giant sandcastles in the soft sand
The mums and dads fetch melting ice creams
Tired and happy they pack their bags
And go home.

Phoebe Eaton (9)
Farleigh School

ROADS

Drivers hooting horns,
Stuck in terrible traffic.
The policeman's siren warns
The crash ahead's horrific.

Infuriating fumes
Irritate my nose.
A sports car zooms
As through the lights it goes.

Loads of lorries roaring
Down the motorway.
Everybody's rushing
Because of the delay.

Why must we go so fast?
Why are we always rushing?
Maybe we'll save at last
This countryside we're crushing.

C J Hanbury-Williams (9)
Farleigh School

THE HAUNTED HOUSE

In the spooky haunted house,
Shivering creatures,
Curses of zombies coming out
From their graves,
Evil dummies thrashing,
Crashing and mumbling,
Skeletons in coffins shaking
And waking.

Guy Wilson (8)
Farleigh School

DOGS

Pets are wonderful
Pets are fun
Dogs are wonderful
Cats are none.

Feed them, love them
Groom them, bath them
Walk them, cuddle them
Oh how loving they are.

Vets can help them
Nurses observe them
Injections, hate them
But chocolates, love them.

Collars can choke them
But chips can find them
Old people miss them and
Young people kiss them.

Fences keep them
Rabbits excite them
Water cools them
But squirrels fool them

Drooling at mealtimes
Begging at other times
Barking at odd times
Whining at night-time.

Pets are excellent
Especially dogs
Young ones are great
Old ones too
Wagging their tails
While loving you, too.

Kate Aroskin (9)
Farleigh School

BURGLARS AT NIGHT

What's that?
Did I hear a noise?
No, it must be the cat.
But I don't have a cat.
Could it be a burglar?
It must be.

Oh no! It sounds like a crash.
It is, it is.
It's the vase!
I must go down and look.
Cr-e-a-k goes the floor.
Who is there?

Creeping silently in the moonlight
Down the stairs, through the hall,
I peek around the door daringly.
My heart goes thump, thump . . .
My ears deceive me.
It is a mystery feline phantom shadow.

Georgia Brooke-Hitching (8)
Farleigh School

SPACE RACE

The judge shouts out,
The crowd shouts aloud,
It's nearly time,
I flick a dime
And *go*.

Flying through the misty stars,
Soaring round the planets,
I'm in the lead,
Nearly light speed.
My engines have gone down,
Oh no, I've lost the crown.

The safety men have come,
I feel so dumb.
They're taking me home,
I feel I'm inside a big cone.
As the twinkling stars go by,
I'm wondering in the starry sky.
What will I do when I return?
I know, from all this I will learn.

As I sit in my quarters here,
As I drink my Carlsberg beer,
Even though I did not win,
I still have my lucky pin.
To see all the twinkling stars
And to think the planets were ours.
Even though I did not win,
I still hear the crowd's din.

Louise Harvey (9)
Farleigh School

I WAS A BIRD

Walking one day
Along the pavement,
A fine sunny day in May,
Suddenly my body started shrinking!
I was completely amazed!
Mouth started bulging wildly out,
Now so full of shock I went into a daze!

Waking up out of this trance
For some reason I felt rather low,
Opening my eyes I took a quick glance
I realised I was a bird; I'm free,
A peregrine falcon to be sure,
Flapping my wings as hard as I could,
Come on, I must flap them more!
With great excitement I left the ground,
Up through a gap in the dark green trees,
Out into the lovely open fresh air,
Faster than a swarm of angry bees.
Up, up higher I went into the open sky.
I flew higher and higher: the sun was lit,
Looking down at the ground below,
Being sure I didn't regret it one bit.

Now going into a glorious dive,
With the wind whipping at my face,
Not too fast I said to myself; I want to come out alive,
Just then I heard an ear-splitting shot
And for some time I painfully bled,
I smacked the ground with a crash
And I was dead.

George Bishop (10)
Farleigh School

WINTER

In my hands a hot cup of tea I hold,
To help me cope with the winter cold,
Jack Frost came at the middle of the night,
Now my windows are frosty white.
You could almost believe it's Christmas Day,
But that just seems so far away.

A little bird scratches at the snow,
To get that worm from down below.
That worm must think he's got no brain,
For there on a table is a pile of grain.

Winter will soon fade away,
Then the year will bring a new spring day.
Flowers and daffodils will soon come out,
That makes me want to jump and shout.
Just like a little baby fawn,
Which has only just been born.

Louisa Eaton (10)
Farleigh School

NIGHT ATTIC

Damp floorboards creaking,
Rats scratching,
Owls hooting,
Bats screeching.

Spooky spiders eating flies,
Dust floating,
Beetles scurrying around,
Rotting wood.

Freddie Few-Brown (8)
Farleigh School

IN THE WILD

In the dark, animals come out,
In the distance you hear children shout.
You awake by cock-a-doodle-do,
Followed by moo moo.
You see deer jump and they
Land with a little delicate thump.
You ride over the countryside,
You see the sun go down to hide.
At night you hear owls hoot,
As you hear little birds toot.
As the moon rises, animals gather in different sizes.

India Cornett (8)
Farleigh School

BONFIRE NIGHT

Outside you can see zooming rockets
Going up to explode
To come down in pieces
Catherine wheels go round and round
Bang goes a Roman candle
Red, green, blue, colours come down in a fall
Zoom, bang, crack
Bangers go eek as they go up
You hold sparklers in your hand
At the end you eat chips.

Laurie Edwards (9)
Farleigh School

NIGHT

In a spooky haunted house
The bats flap,
The doors creak and the rats
Screech.

Outside the trees are still
As night,
The owls hoot like a horn
Being blown over the silent night,
Rivers shimmer as the silver moon
Looks down.

Johnnie Sinclair (8)
Farleigh School

MY NIGHT POEM

Owls hooting, foxes hunting,
    Moon waning,
Wind whistling, mice
    Scurrying silently,
Moon glimmering on
    The stream.

Edward Orlik (8)
Farleigh School

I AM FRIGHTENED!

Sometimes I lie in bed at night,
Listening for the sound of bats
Flying around the room.
I feel scared!

Thoughts enter my head,
Of shadows watching over me,
Of spiders falling on me from
Creepy strings.

James Clifton (8)
Farleigh School

AT THE MOVIE

At the movie lots of things are going on
People waiting in a queue for food
Children jumping up and down
Mums chatting with their friends
Teens are eating popcorn
Dads are on their phones
Music is drifting outside
Yummy smells are coming from the kitchen
At the movie, what's going on?

Charly Kilkenny (8)
Farleigh School

FIREWORKS

All of a sudden there was whiz, boom and bang,
The Catherine wheels go shhhhhh.
The bonfire crackles as steam goes shooting up in the air.
As the fireworks of whiz, boom, bang, the dogs howl, cats miaow.
Hot dogs are lovely to eat but the ketchup goes every way.
Guy Fawkes is made out of my dad's old clothes
And stuffed with straw.

Harry Hensman (8)
Farleigh School

TURTLES

Turtles scurry across the beach,
I really do hope they don't screech.
Swimming through the water,
With their short stubby legs.
Cautiously hiding,
Suspiciously guiding.

Buried eggs in the sand,
Greenhouses over their heads.
Long claws that push them through the water,
I hope they have at least one daughter.

Charlotte Liebling (8)
Farleigh School

BADGERS AT NIGHT

Badgers are night
Crawling along the ground
Looking for something to eat
Shy badgers, looking around cautiously
Nice badgers, talking to the wild animals
Happy badgers, smiling secretly
Sad badgers, crying
Cute badgers, with sweet faces
Lovely badgers and
Fluffy badgers too!

Anna Fabian (8)
Farleigh School

WANTED

He has a small beard
Which looks very weird
He is very tall and thin
He has a cheesy grin.

He's in a lot of trouble
No, make that double!
I am happy to say
£10 million could be given today.

If you find him
Definitely hand him in
Collect your money
And let the fun begin!

Lucy Jack (10)
Fernhurst Junior School

THE DRAGON

It's purple and green,
It's big and fat.
It's evil and mean,
It could eat your cat!

It lives in a cave,
It sleeps on stones.
Its name is Dave,
It is a dragon!

Danielle Dore (9)
Fernhurst Junior School

AT THE RAILWAY TRACK

I was at the railway track,
I saw a big black sack.
I saw my train coming,
Something in the bag was humming.

I opened it up to look inside
And suddenly to my surprise,
There was a child,
She said she lived in the wild.

I took her back to the wild,
I saw another child.
I thought, what are they doing?
I said, 'What are you chewing?'

Rebecca Wateridge (10)
Fernhurst Junior School

THERE ONCE WAS A MOUSE

There once was a tiny mouse
Who lived in a tiny house.
It shuffled all day,
I hope it doesn't stay.

In the little tiny house,
Where there once lived a mouse,
Sometimes I think I would
Catch him if I really could!

Charlotte Chase (9)
Fernhurst Junior School

AUTUMN

Autumn days when
the blackberries
grow and all the
leaves fall to the
ground. Yellow
leaves are falling
one by one and
leaves so crunchy
when you walk
all over them.
Leaves go flying
in the wind and
the wind's so strong
that it pushes you
back when you're
trying to walk to
school. You better
wrap up warm
before you go
to school because
you might just get
a cold.

Stuart Asseter (11)
Knights Enham Junior School

THE SEA POETRY

I must go down the sea again,
To feed the dolphins and whales
And ride on them,
To hear them whine
And to care for them.

Kayleigh MacDonald (10)
Knights Enham Junior School

COLOURS OF THE WORLD

Y is for the yellow sparkling in the sun.
B is for the blueness in the sea.
G is for the greenness in the grass.
R is for the red in the rose.
P is for the purple in the pansies.
O is for the orange in the tingling fire.
W is for the white in the snow.
T is for the terracotta in the fruits.
P is for the pink in the flowers.
L is for the lime in the wallpaper.
G is for the goldness in the gates to Heaven.
S is for the silver in the twinkling stars.
B is for the blackness in the thunder clouds.
C is for all the colours in the world.

Joanne Richardson (10)
Knights Enham Junior School

THE CAPTAIN

Although I am the captain
  I do my work
So that will be my work
  For the day
But when I wake up
  I'm all ready again

And when I sail the seas
  I see the boats come in
From the sea, so when you see me
  I will be sailing the seas.

Lewis Muir (11)
Knights Enham Junior School

THE PATH THROUGH MY LIFE

As I walked along the road
    I could see,
Forward in my path,
    My destiny.

As I walked along the road
    I could see,
A field on my right,
    To my left, a tree.

As I walked along the road
    I could hear,
The tune of my past,
    Dancing in my ear.

Life is a path which will eventually end,
    So enjoy your walk,
    Through every bend.

Anne-Marie Jamieson (11)
Knights Enham Junior School

UNCLE BOB

My uncle is so thick
My uncle is bald
My uncle has a weird name
My uncle snores in his sleep
My uncle has no teeth
My uncle needs to be fed
My uncle can't walk
Uncle Bob, what can you do?

Colin Hughes (11)
Knights Enham Junior School

PRINCE CHARMING

Prince Charming is getting bored
Of sitting in the palace alone,
The pretty young man wants a wife
And if he finds the right girl
And she says 'Oh yes my lovely prince'
Then the prince is going to have a ball.

So if you want to sit on the royal throne,
Don't stay at home, dress yourself up in
                              your best clothes
And come to the palace at 8 o'clock,
Don't miss the chance,
It could be you
At the engagement dance!

Luke James (11)
Knights Enham Junior School

FLOWERS

F   is for the blue sky of the fairy flaxes in the summer.
L   is for the pink lilies in the green field in the summer.
O   is for the pink orchid sitting in your garden on the green grass.
W   is for the pink rosebay willow-herbs in the forest.
E   is for the white enchanter-nightshade in the flower pot.
R   is for the red sunset of the rose.
S   is for the yellow sun of the stonecrop in the summer field.

Faye Jones (11)
Knights Enham Junior School

THE BEGGAR

Alone in the corner, the old beggar sits,
waiting for someone to speak to her.
She lurks in the shadows, ready to pounce,
waiting for her long lost love.

Two cupped hands, a black woollen shawl,
an old croaky voice saying, 'A penny for a pauper.'
Her grey hair blows around in the wind,
her pale, careworn face stays the same.

The diligent citizens bustle past in an air of confusion,
not stopping, not looking, not bothering at all.
Too engrossed in their own busy lives.

Alone in the corner, the old beggar sits,
waiting, waiting,
for something that will never come.

Louise Silke (10)
Knights Enham Junior School

HEAR THEM CRY

I must go down to the sea again
To see the sunset
And hear the whales cry
To say goodnight to their
Lonely friends
That are away from them.

Stephanie Louise Smith (11)
Knights Enham Junior School

MY BIG OAK TREE

My big oak tree is big and brown,
All the leaves are still there now.
I can't believe it's still big after a century,
    But how can it survive?
    Is it cursed? I don't know.
My oak tree has leaves that grow,
But they have all gone now!
My big oak tree is big and brown
And whoops! It just fell down!
So then I got my plough to move it!
It was only yesterday, I only just bought one
                                    to plant today!

Sam Gray (10)
Knights Enham Junior School

AUTUMN

It's autumn and time to wrap up warm,
Crackling fires and roasted chestnuts,
Longer at night, shorter at day,
People are crying 'Go away! Go away!'
Now it is time to say our goodbyes to the long summer days
And the short roasting nights,
Now it is time to welcome autumn,
The crimson leaves laid stricken across the dewed grass.
Autumn good morning,
Summer goodnight.

Lindsey Taylor (10)
Knights Enham Junior School

MY BROTHER

My brother has no eyes,
My brother is hairy,
My brother is dumb,
My brother is ugly,
My brother comes from Mars,
My brother is weird,
My brother can't walk or talk,
My brother is a space boy,
My brother's name is Gurgle,
My brother likes the 60s,
My brother snores in his sleep,
But he likes to count sheep,
What can he do?
I think he's an alien.

Ashley Amphlett (11)
Knights Enham Junior School

BUSY BEES

Bees, bees, busy bees,
Buzz their way to town
Bees, bees, busy bees,
Collect their honey and nectar
Bees, bees, busy bees,
Love their queen and honey
Bees, bees, busy bees
Have a princess almighty
Bees, bees, busy bees
Look how they dance and play
Bees, bees, busy bees,
Look how they mooch around.

Ashley Ritson (10)
Knights Enham Junior School

AUTUMN HAS COME

The autumn leaves
So big and shiny,
They race along,
As they go by,
The faster they run,
The faster they go,
They won't be able to stop.
Leaves, leaves, leaves, leaves,
I just can't stop going on about leaves,
Because I love them so much
And I wish autumn would never go away
And when I sleep I hear them scrape and weave.

Luke Richardson (10)
Knights Enham Junior School

WALKING DOWN THE LANE

I was walking down the lane,
I saw someone called McBain,
He said he had a gun,
So I turned around to run.

He stopped to grab a bun,
He said he's having fun,
I said go home to your mum.

He went home to his mum,
She smacked his bum
For being so late
In the afternoon!

C J Tee (10)
Knights Enham Junior School

DAYS OF NATURE

Today the birds will scatter,
Tomorrow doesn't matter.
Now the birds will sing,
As night is drawing in.

Today the wind will blow,
Tomorrow, I don't know.
Now the wind will spread its wing,
As night is drawing in.

Today the bees do fly,
Tomorrow, blue will be the sky.
Now the bees are sharpening their stings,
As night is drawing in.

Today the sun does shine,
Tomorrow will be mine.
Now the sun is dying,
As night is drawing in.

Today the moon wears a mask,
Tomorrow I dare to ask.
Now the moon is coming,
As night is drawing in.

Today you read this poem,
Tomorrow you will be going.
Now you must do the opposite of begin,
As night is drawing in.

Amy Whittall (10)
Knights Enham Junior School

ICE CREAM, ICE CREAM

Ice cream
Ice cream
That's all I like
Ice cream
Ice cream
I eat it on my bike
Ice cream
Ice cream
I eat it with my ted
Ice cream
Ice cream
It fell in the stream
Ice cream
Ice cream
I just have to scream
Ice cream
Ice cream
It's fallen in the stream
Ice cream
Ice cream
I wish it was still here with me
Ice cream
Ice cream
It still loves me, probably.

Luke Buckwell (10)
Knights Enham Junior School

INTERGALACTIC SPACE DOG 2050
LOST IN THE GALAXY

In the back garden, having fun,
A cat's on the wall, run! Run! Run!
Up on the space shuttle onto the wall,
Watch out cat, it's your call.
Rocket boosters on to reach the cat,
Rocket boosters out of fuel, oh dog food, oh rats.
Cat disappears, I'm far out of town,
Ah oh! Oh no, I'm really stuck now.
Meteor rocks are falling from the sky,
I have the feeling I might die!
I'm running! I'm running as fast as I can,
All the way home to my owner's, my man.

Jessica Bradley (11)
Micheldever CP School

I DON'T WANT TO GO!

'We're going to the sea and the sand.'
'I don't want to go!'
'Come on! Come on! We're going to play netball
On the shiny, silky sand.'
'I don't want to go!'
'Please, pretty please,' said Mum and Dad.
'You can have ice creams, a donkey ride or even
Watch Punch and Judy!'
Donkey ride? Punch and Judy?
'I do want to go, I do, I do, I do!
Please can I go, please, pretty please.'
'Yes, you can! Come on!'

Erin Canny (10)
Micheldever CP School

THE PEACEMAKER!

There's the stress of a Monday afternoon lingering,
I'm wearing a blue and gold badge to show my importance.

Children are shouting, fighting and biting!

I'm trying to sort out arguments which make no sense.
Talking through problems, listening to them,
Children are screaming about who goes first.

Children are shouting, fighting and biting!

Can't shout I'll probably scare them!
My friends are falling out,
Oh no, I try to sort it out.
Some infants run to me with their tell-tales.

Children are shouting, fighting and biting!

That's a peacemaker's life!
Beware of it!

Rachel Flenley (10)
Micheldever CP School

SNITCH THE SPIDER

Slowly Snitch the spider scuttles out of his web,
Carefully, cleverly, creeping towards his prey,
As he does every day,
Shivering as he snatches the fearful prey,
He wraps, squeezes and crushes it in his jaws,
The fine fiddly thread shakes in the breeze,
As Snitch, silently, slowly slides to the centre of his den.

Jack Ballard (11)
Micheldever CP School

ALLITERATIVE 'S'

Six singing sloths slowly swinging on the swings,
Seven slithering snakes slide slowly,
Sixteen spiky spiders smelling seafood stuffed with spuds,
Seventeen slinking slugs slithering in the soil,
Sixty startled stags saving sisters in Scottish lands,
Seventy sleek seals swimming slowly in the stormy seas,
Seventy-seven snails sliding slowly on Swanage shores,
Six hundred souls saved by savages,
Seven hundred scorpions stinging stylish sailors,
Six thousand swans hissing scarily in Sweden,
Seven thousand sharks sliding silently through seas,
Six hundred thousand silly sheep being sheared in sheds,
Seven hundred thousand sticklebacks swimming in the Seven.
Stop Ss - I'm sick of you!

Joanne Bell (11)
Micheldever CP School

MY SPECIAL PET

Looks like a worm,
It can be taken anywhere,
It has a blue coat,
It's very quiet,
It will fit anywhere,
Long hair,
You don't have to feed,
Slithers everywhere,
It does not make a mess,
It doesn't die,
Held on a string,
It does what I want.

Dean Seddon (10)
Micheldever CP School

HATS EVERYWHERE!

Tall hats, small hats,
Caps for naps,
Naps for caps,
Lots of hats,
Any hats,
Hurray for a hat!

Straw hats, more hats,
Australian cork hats,
Piggy pork hats,
Lots of hats,
Any hats,
Hurray for a hat!

Simple hats for summer,
Woolly hats of winter,
Hats for cats,
Hats for bats!
Hurray for a hat!

Donkey hats, wonky hats,
Swimming hats,
Clown hats,
Lots of hats,
Any hats,
Hurray for a hat!

Old hats, worn hats,
Smelly hats, new hats,
Lots of hats,
Any hats,
Hurray for a hat!

Rosanna Sutcliffe (9)
Micheldever CP School

SUNSET

Sunset, shades of red,
Orange, peach and yellow,
We watch with empty heads,
Dreaming silently.

Happy, warm-hearted,
We see light, wispy clouds,
Romantic streaks of colour,
Sun sent from the gods,
A golden chariot across the sky.

Down in Oz, the sun is bright,
A huge, dazzling ball.
Back in England, we sleep through the night.

Zoe Anderson (9)
Micheldever CP School

LIZZIE LIZARD

Lizzie Lizard, lazy and green,
lies on a leaf,
soaking up the sun.
Her long tongue shoots out to catch her prey;
she has dry, rough skin,
she sheds her skin quite often;
heavy on my hand,
with her long, soft, sensitive tail.
She climbs quickly up every wall,
unafraid of heights;
black, shiny, oval eyes
with yellow pupils,
she looks at me freakily.

Gregory King (9)
Micheldever CP School

SPACE SHUTTLE

Ready for launch,
In the shuttle,
We have ignition,
Fiery boosters,
All in smoke.

We're in the air,
Through the atmosphere,
Space shuttle in space,
Orbiting Earth,
Entering asteroid belt.

Planet ahead,
Veer off course,
Just miss planet,
Asteroid hits shuttle,
Shuttle blows up.

Chris Knight-Jones (9)
Micheldever CP School

A JOURNEY OF LIFE

She was born at dawn
Mum thought she was a play-baby
Dad thought she was a moddler-toddler
Then she was a teenager
Then she was a mother
And she got married
And had her own baby
And she was a grandma
Then she got to 84, she died.

Hannah Carvall (8)
Milford-On-Sea Primary School

SNAKE POEM

Slimy, slithering snakes,
Long tongue dangling to the ground,
Basking in the sun all day long,
Catching mice, yum, yum, yum.

Kelly Tucker (8)
Milford-On-Sea Primary School

A BOY IN FRANCE

There was a boy from France
Who was trying to dance
A plane flew past
Made him spin so fast
That poor dizzy boy in France.

Wade Fisher (8)
Milford-On-Sea Primary School

SNAKE

Slimy, scaly, slithering snake
Climbing up the slippery rake!
Fell down with a bump
Slithered home with a lump!
Seriously thought, 'Oh no!
Silly me, lost a toe.'

Charlotte Gates (8)
Milford-On-Sea Primary School

TIGERS

Tigers are silly, tigers are rough
Tigers are hard, tigers can scratch
Tigers fight and hunt down their prey
Tigers can roar, tigers can play
Tigers are frightening when
They pounce
But I really like tigers.

Craig Foot (7)
Milford-On-Sea Primary School

A FLOWER

I'm a little seed,
Sitting in the ground,
Not making a sound,
Here's a tiny shoot,
Oh look! Here's a root,
Out comes a flower,
Bringing all its glamour.

Laura Wilkins (8)
Milford-On-Sea Primary School

THERE WAS A YOUNG BOY FROM MARS

There was a young boy from Mars,
Who wanted to play with the stars,
He took off in his rocket,
Kept mice in his pocket
And candy in big coloured jars!

Oliver Hill (8)
Milford-On-Sea Primary School

MONKEY

I'm a funky monkey,
I'm not very lumpy.
I swing from tree to tree
And I nearly got hit by a bee.
I'm furry and curly,
I go *ooheehoohoo!*
That's because
I'm a funky monkey.

Frank Short
Milford-On-Sea Primary School

SNAKES

Slimy snakes slither and slide
Hissing loud
Curling up tight
In a big circle
They will be
Hiding in grass
From you and me.

Hannah Clark (9)
Milford-On-Sea Primary School

A FRESH START

Making a fresh start,
You have to be good at heart,
Be kind and willing,
It's very thrilling,
To have a new head
Like you!

April Doyle (8)
Milford-On-Sea Primary School

THE NIGHTMARE

A zombie is coming after me,
Round the corner, round the bend,
Whether he eats me it depends,
But it's probably the bitter end.

Velociraptor's angry,
I've pinched her egg,
Rows of razor sharp teeth,
Encircling round my head.

Alien on his UFO,
That squishy, squashy thing
Is surely going to kill me,
I'm tied to a table,
Sharp spike hangs above,
Thankfully I wake up,
Back to reality,
. . . *Or is it?*

Patrick Bettle (9)
Milford-On-Sea Primary School

MONSTERS

There's a monster in the attic
With horns as thick as pipe.
It lives in the graveyard
It fills me with fear.
I don't know when it's coming
Or when it's really near.
When am I
Going to get out of here
And think of ginger beer?

William Clark (8)
Milford-On-Sea Primary School

LITTLE PUPPIES

Little puppies all alone
Mum and Dad - they aren't home.
Robbers broke in through the door
And stole us puppies from the floor.
The policeman said, 'We will find them soon.'
Mum and Dad called out to the moon.
Robbers hid us in Cruella de Ville's house.
We sneaked out through a hole,
A bit bigger than a mouse.
Through field and ditch, sleet and snow,
We finally found the way to go.
Back safe and sound with Mum and Dad,
What a time we all have had!

Katherine Cooper (8)
Milford-On-Sea Primary School

HAVE YOU EVER BEEN ON A GHOST TRAIN?

Have you ever been on a ghost train,
You'll regret it if you have,
There's witches' cats
And scary bats,
Howling, growling monsters!
Rattling skeletons too,
Loooook ouuuuuuttt!
Oh - boo hoo hoo!
If you haven't been on a ghost train . . .

Don't!

Sara Wallis (8)
Milford-On-Sea Primary School

JOURNEY THROUGH LIFE

I was born at dawn,
On Christmas morn.
Mark said maybe I'm a baby,
Mum said I was an odd todd,
Dad shouted out, 'She's a very mild school child.'
I'm major when I'm a teenager,
My children are a bother when I'm a mother.
I'm a grandmother, my grandchildren's teacher is Mrs Suther.
I lied when I died.

Mia Kett (8)
Milford-On-Sea Primary School

A JOURNEY THROUGH LIFE

She was born at dawn
Mum said, 'She's maybe a girl baby.'
Dad said, 'She's a moddler-toddler.'
She's a wild school child.
The teacher said, 'She's a major teenager.'
She's just like my other mother,
She's a grandparent like Mrs Slerant,
She sighed before she died.

Francesca Douglas (8)
Milford-On-Sea Primary School

TOUCH

Touch is the warmth of the fire
As your hands stretch out

Touch is a snowflake melting
On your tongue

Touch is the silky carpet of
Grass under your feet

Touch is the sand slipping
Through your fingers.

Zoe Adam (7)
Milford-On-Sea Primary School

ICICLES

Rock hard icicles like sharp teeth,
Melting minute by minute,
Ice cream comes but transparent ones,
A frosty feeling: icicles in the cold, long winter,
Icicles, cold like sharp knives cutting your fingers!
You touch the end and you shall be cursed
By the coldness of *icicles!*

Katie Osborne (7)
Milford-On-Sea Primary School

A FLYING BIRD

Goes when it's too cold
Comes back to the nest when hot
When the bird starts to fly it spreads its wings out
Flies like a speedboat on the water
The bird would fly down to get some food
Flying over sea breams and ice creams
And cries while flies
He spreads his wings in spring
Then after the journey of life, it cries and dies.

Daniel Martin (8)
Milford-On-Sea Primary School

A JOURNEY THOUGH OUR LIFE

Every one of us starts as a newborn baby,
I wonder if you're one too?
You have not stopped growing
Yet you need to be a toddler.
Then here comes the hard bit,
School, boring.
Now let me see, oh yes then you're a teenager.
Oh dear then you meet somebody
And you become a family
And you need to clear up after your family.
Then you get old and you get white or grey hair.
Then you start being a grandma or a grandad
And you start to baby-sit.
Then you get really, really old
And be a great grandma or grandad.
Then this is the sad bit,
You die.

Betsy Jennings (8)
Milford-On-Sea Primary School

THE JUNGLE KING

The jungle king
Is rough and tough
He sneaks through trees
He squeezes through bushes
What is he?

A lion!

Jessica Steel (8)
Milford-On-Sea Primary School

SNOW

Soft, silky snow upon your hand,
Sparkling snow drifting down from the sky.
Looking up gives you a happy feeling,
But coldness when you look down.
Snow tinkles from your hand,
Freezing, fluffy flakes falling from the sky.
Shivering fingers, freezing as ice,
Silent snow on the ground,
People shivering all around.
Snow that flutters down like confetti at a wedding,
People treading on crisp, chunky snow,
Sparkling, crystals of ice.

Jess Merivale (8)
Milford-On-Sea Primary School

IN THE JUNGLE

In the jungle the trees I pass
The snakes and tigers hide in grass.
The oaks fall on the ground
The tigers roar and then they pound.

I come to a gate and the monkeys are eating bananas,
I walk through the gate and see Indians lighting a fire.

I walk past the Indians and come to an end,
I walk through a path that really does bend.
The wind starts to blow
And I come to the end of a great journey.

James Nash (8)
Milford-On-Sea Primary School

THE BIG, BIG FLOWER

A mousy in the desert was walking to and fro
When he saw a big, big flower,
He tasted a petal, it tasted very sour.
When he went past the big, big flower
He found he was lost.
He tried to look for the flower
But he said, 'Why am I lost?'

Alison Hall (7)
Milford-On-Sea Primary School

THERE WAS AN OLD LADY FROM SPAIN

There was an old lady from Spain
She liked to play in the rain
An aeroplane flew past
And landed on the grass
And she was never seen again.

Christopher Humm (8)
Milford-On-Sea Primary School

A COBRA

Smoothly slithering on his scaly skin,
Up and around the smelly bin.
His fangs are sharp to attack its prey,
Careful, you might be on its menu today!

Lloyd Woodford (9)
Milford-On-Sea Primary School

A BEE'S JOURNEY

A bee goes to collect its nectar,
   He gets it from a flower.
They live in groups of five
   In a bee hive.
They fly somewhere every day,
   Busy, busy in every way.
When someone makes them angry they sting
   And then dance and sing.
They fly from flower to flower with their bee power.
   A bee makes his honey and thinks it's very funny.

Amelia Sutton (8)
Milford-On-Sea Primary School

A BEE

A bee lives in a hive,
If they sting then it will die.
Their colour is black and yellow,
Looks like a soft marshmallow.
They fly all day from day to day,
They make a funny noise when they fly
And collect pollen to make sweet honey.
So they fly flower to flower
And fly up a tower to make sweet honey.
Lovely, lovely honey,
It costs lots of money.

Abbie Parrish (8)
Milford-On-Sea Primary School

A JOURNEY IN A CAR

They put the key in the keyhole and start the engine and get ready to go.
The children wave and shout as other cars go past the window.
The children playing I spy and reading a book.
Soon they are sound asleep, nothing to disturb them except for a beep.
Beeeep! Now that woke them, now they're crying.
Soon they stop and back to playing I spy.
The children fidgeting and fighting, Mum soon stops the argument.
They look out the window and start to get bored.
We are near home now but the children don't speak, they are
                                                     sound asleep.

Alastair Caldwell (8)
Milford-On-Sea Primary School

A JOURNEY TO FRANCE

Going to the ferry port,
Seeing the cars going in the ferries.
Seeing the ferries go out to sea.
Seeing the ferries coming in to port.
Seeing the cars come out of the ferries.
Seeing the waves rushing behind the boat.
Seeing the dock ahead of you makes you feel glad.

Nathan Prince (8)
Milford-On-Sea Primary School

DAYS WITHOUT DRAGONS

I'm glad I live in modern days,
Now dragons aren't around,
I like to live in modern ways,
As dragons don't make a sound,
I'm glad dragons were just a phase.

I'm glad I live in modern days,
Now I cannot be scared,
Scared to be in a maze,
Or to lose the way,
I'm glad dragons aren't a craze.

Simon Halliday (9)
Milford-On-Sea Primary School

MODERN DAYS

It's good I live in days of new,
We've got computers,
PS2,
I'm glad that I am part of it,
So many things that I can do.

It's good I live in days of new,
The cinema,
The snooker cue,
I hope that it'll stay this way,
At least till 2002!

Duncan Bradley (10)
Milford-On-Sea Primary School

SENSES

I love the smell of fresh bread.
I love the taste of red-hot pizza.
I love the feeling of my warm soft pillow.
I love the sound of the honeybee's wings.
I love the sight of trees in spring.

Sam Clark (9)
Milford-On-Sea Primary School

A Journey In A Car

The key in the engine, we're going to go,
Give your hugs and kisses before we go.

Children playing in the back of the car
And say 'Is it going to be far?'

Playing I spy and card games as well,
The children think it's swell.

Grown-ups chatting all day long,
While the children sing a beautiful song.

Finally the journey has stopped and most are fast asleep
And not a peep.

Rhys Roberts (9)
Milford-On-Sea Primary School

Butterflies

Butterflies collecting pollen from flowers
It is very sweet
They are very pretty
They are all different colours
As quiet as anything
Pink, yellow, purple to very pretty colours
When it is cold they fly somewhere else
First I was a caterpillar but now I'm a beautiful butterfly
Wings like silk
Flying around day to day.

Chloe Jeffcock (8)
Milford-On-Sea Primary School

A SPARROW'S WINTER

Sparrow fly like arrows,
Fast across the Earth.
Feeding on worms and insects
Like flies as they fly high in the blue, blue sky.
Trying not to be caught by bigger birds,
Like hawks or Chinese people throwing forks.
The sparrow flies away because of the snowy season
And everyone in England should know the reason.
The parent sparrows fly their children to countries
Like France to let them stay with others like their uncles or aunts.
When the parents give birth they pick up their children
And fly back to the other side of the Earth
When it is warm again.

Dean Perriton (8)
Milford-On-Sea Primary School

AN ANT'S JOURNEY

It was searching for some food
When a fly swept out of the blue
It took me to its den in America
The ant was high in the sky
He got dropped high on a cliff top
He couldn't hear his mum calling his name
He couldn't smell his supper
He sees a bee which took him above trees and seas
He went against the sun which made him get a tan
He got home and went to bed.

Danyel Cleall (9)
Milford-On-Sea Primary School

THE 21ST CENTURY

I wish to stay in the 21st century
Where things are better planned.
Where the olden days I think were temporary
And I'm glad that now we have the Queen
And not the old King Henry.

I wish to stay in the 21st century
With better things to do,
With a two pound coin, not just the penny.
Without the dragons chasing to eat you,
With lots more houses by far.

Sandy Crawford (11)
Milford-On-Sea Primary School

GROOVY YEARS

I'm pleased I live in the modern years,
Where Tate Modern has just opened
And where the government stops our tears.
There are smoke alarms to keep us safe
And in the woods you might find a deer.

I'm pleased I live in the modern years,
But the Millennium Dome has just shut
Because of the government I have no fears.
Lots of people learn to drive,
That's why I like the modern years.

Bryony Hull (10)
Milford-On-Sea Primary School

MODERN DAYS, THE DIFFERENCE BETWEEN OLD AND NEW

I'm pleased I live in modern days,
Where dragons don't live,
Now dragons aren't the rage,
I'm very glad indeed,
Because I enjoy the days.

I'm pleased I live in modern days,
Where magic isn't the rage,
You still have legends being told,
People are brave,
People are still bold.

Henry Crofts (11)
Milford-On-Sea Primary School

MODERN DAYS

I wish I could stay in modern days,
Where magic isn't here,
We can laze,
Without the dragons roaming,
We can gaze.

I wish I could stay in modern days,
Without brave knights that fight
And I'm glad that computers are the craze,
I'm glad that we have shops
And that we keep to the government's ways.

Rebecca Cooper (11)
Milford-On-Sea Primary School

A JOURNEY TO THE MOON

Many things go on a journey
but this particular one
circles round the Earth
and it's opposite the sun

The moon travels on its orbit
round the Earth all night
it reflects the sun's light rays
so it's very, very bright

Have you ever heard of Neil Armstrong?
He was the first man on the moon
landed in 1969
he was on the moon at noon.

Louise Darley (8)
Milford-On-Sea Primary School

MODERN DAYS

I'm glad I lived in modern days
When football was in fashion
I like to use modern ways
By watching television
I always struggled in a maze
But I still got praise

I'm glad I lived in modern days
Playing football every week
When people were lying on the bays
When I had lots of friends
While my dad kept my sisters amazed.

James Winderam (9)
Milford-On-Sea Primary School

A JOURNEY TO GREECE!

Packing our cases
With smiles on our faces
It is four in the morning
Taxis and yawning
Queuing
Waiting
Passports
The plane is in!
Eating our sweets
Finding our seats
Oh good
We're off now!
Engines roaring
The house is shrinking
What a lovely time for thinking.

Elizabeth Shearing (8)
Milford-On-Sea Primary School

MODERN DAY

I miss the olden days
Here they have roaring monsters, I heard someone call cars
I hate the modern ways
Here the world's round not flat
The village is a maze

I miss the olden days
Here they have big snakes that make loud noises
Why are those ladies lying on the bays?
Here people have jewels in their tongues and holes in their noses
I just can't wait to go home and play.

Sasha Flatau (9)
Milford-On-Sea Primary School

SHRINKING

My name is Mable, I'm sitting on the table,
I think I'm shrinking, I'm sure, I'm sure I'm not drinking.
I think I might drop at the sight of my tiny head,
I don't deserve this life,
It's complete and utter strife.
Oh wow, I think I'm here
And not a single tear.
Look, there's a tiny mouse,
In its little house.
Oh no, it's coming near,
I think I'll have a tear.
Oh yes, I'm growing again,
Do you think I will now be ten?
Hello Mum, hello Dad,
You're the things that make me glad.

Emily Underwood (8)
Milford-On-Sea Primary School

I'M GLAD I LIVE IN MODERN DAYS

I'm glad I live in modern days
When everybody goes to school
When we go out to the field to play
And everything is dead cool
But we still have to do what the teacher says
I'm glad I live in the modern days
When astronauts go into space
You go on the beach, the sandy bays
Your dad goes to work carrying his suitcase
I'm glad I live in the modern days.

Sophie Withers (9)
Milford-On-Sea Primary School

COMPUTER DAYS

I'm glad I live in computer days
When dragons don't exist,
When I walk across the bays
I wonder why
Dragons got their ways

I'm glad I live in modern times
Watching TV all night
I watch the skateboards do some grinds
Then I have my lunch
Whilst listening to my chimes.

Jack Murphy (10)
Milford-On-Sea Primary School

MODERN DAYS

I'm glad I live in the modern days
Where there's a lot of technology
I like to live in modern ways
There's supermarkets and shops
Like Tescos and Safeways.

Jack Ferrar (10)
Milford-On-Sea Primary School

MODERN YEARS

I'm glad I live in modern days
Because of computers, cars and toys
They're fun, fun and cool in every way
Websites are fun and you have food in your tummy
Technology is here to stay.

Jake Shepherd (10)
Milford-On-Sea Primary School

MODERN DAYS

I'm glad I live in modern days
Because I can fly on a plane
There's something we can say
But hey, let's go and play
We can play a game or two
Join in, there are a few who want to play
I'm glad I live in modern days
Because I can go on a train
And we can play today.

Yasmin Byford (10)
Milford-On-Sea Primary School

MODERN DAYS

I'm happy I live in modern days
Because there are so many activities
And I have lots of sports I play
Golf and football are my favourites
And I play on my PlayStation a lot.

Luke Benford (10)
Milford-On-Sea Primary School

I'D LIKE TO BE

I want to be a cloud floating in the sky
I want to be a cloud up really high
Just lying on my back relaxing in the sun
Oh wouldn't that be fun

I'd love to be a butterfly flying from flower to flower
I'd love to be a butterfly resting every hour
I'd love to be a bee, but then again I just like being me!

Rebecca Knight (8)
Milford-On-Sea Primary School

A JOURNEY THROUGH A CLOUD

I am going on a journey through a cloud,
I wonder how I'll get there?
Maybe I could go on a flying bear?

Mum, it's really cool up here,
I have no fear.
It's turning grey,
I want to stay and play.
I start to bounce around,
It's a long way from the ground.
Don't look
  D
  O
  W
  N.
Oops I fell
  D
  O
  W
  N.
I am back on the ground.
It was fun up there
And what about the flying bear?
Are you there?

Iain Howarth (8)
Milford-On-Sea Primary School

THE BATHROOM SWAMP

I'm going on a journey
I really can't wait
I'm going in the bathroom swamp
It's going to be just great

The food is not nice
Courgettes and cabbage
But I can't tell Mum
Cause she is a savage

I'm going for a shower
Under the waterfall
I haven't got a towel
So I have to use my shawl

I'm going to get in trouble
But I don't care, I'm hungry
I'll have to eat my chocolate bar
Saved for emergencies

I've been here a day
I want to go to bed
I want to rest my aching head
I want to rest my head

Goodbye bathroom swamp
I'll be here again
But next time I'll be fully armed
With 40 thousand men.

Jenny Clark (8)
Milford-On-Sea Primary School

THE BEDROOM JOURNEY!

I'm going on a journey
I just can't wait
I'm going on a journey
I'm sure it will be great
I'd let my teddy drive me there
But he's a bear you see
So he can't drive my little car
Up the mountain for me
I'm gonna get some plungers
Just in case I fall
But then again I could use
My very strong dad, Paul
I'll walk up to the mighty top
And look at the view all day
It's February now, when I come down
I expect it will be May
I'm gonna walk up the wall
(That's the mountain)
It looks really tall
I better not run because
I've got plungers but . . .
It's gonna be fun, I'm going up
The bunk bed that's where I'm
Gonna put the tent
Or shall I use the shed instead
Of the bunk bed?
Ahh a bear *help*
Don't put me there
Don't you dare *ouch* my head!
I'm safe in my bed.

Natassja Shiner (9)
Milford-On-Sea Primary School

THE MODERN AGE

I'm glad I live in the modern age,
With computers still around,
You can post, e-mail, send and page,
With your feet safe on the ground,
So you don't have a rage.

Tom Hill (10)
Milford-On-Sea Primary School

MY CHRISTMAS TREE

Angel
at   the
top, baubles all
around,   lights up
and down, angel are you lonely?
I
hope
not!

Francesca Benoist (7)
Oliver's Battery CP School

ROCKETS

Boom! Zoom!
Rockets whizzing past
And banging in the midnight sky.
Lots of colours fill the sky.
They dash in the air
And at the last big bang
Everyone goes home.

Tom Sanders (8)
Oliver's Battery CP School

CATHERINE WHEEL

A colourful wheel round and round
Squeals from girls, shouts and screams
The bright colours, gold, lime, blue then a navy
Smoke and sparks rising, dogs barking
Cats miaowing, eyes gazing
People laughing
Bangs, whizzes, pops! People gazing and gazing
Excited for the next one.

Matthew Jelliffe (8)
Oliver's Battery CP School

COLOURS

Red is like a big bumpy heart,
Blue is like water dripping from the sky,
Green is like leaves dropping from the tree,
Yellow is like the big bright sun,
Black is like a dark, blank telly.

Ella Ritchie (7)
Pennington Junior School

A COLOUR POEM

Blue is like the fresh air in the sky,
Bright light and calm,
Peaceful, happy.
Blue is like a plant growing from the ground,
That is the sky with little white clouds.
Red is the colour of a shining rose,
A volcano bubbling like a fizzy drink.

Siân Wright (8)
Pennington Junior School

DOGS

The dog is fluffy.
The dog is happy.
The dog is barking.
The dog is good.
The dog is sad.
The dog is glad.
The dog is mad.
The dog needs a bone.

Haydn Rickman (8)
Pennington Junior School

A MEAT-EATER

A meat-eater
Enormous
Very scaly
Sharp teeth
And very scary
Dead!

Billie Maguire (8)
Pennington Junior School

THE DOG

I went to go and see
A dog called Puddles,
He was fluffy,
I had to take him home,
I was good,
He was fluffy!

Marie Townsend (7)
Pennington Junior School

SPACE

Planets are all sorts of shapes
The Earth is mainly meadows and sea.
The stars are glimmering in the pitch-black,
The moon is shining white and light.
The sun is fire burning bright,
If you go near, bang, bang, you're gone.

On my trip through space,
I just saw stars,
Wait! Wait! There's a moon glimmering in the dark.
Boring old stars again.
Wait! Wait! I see the planet Mars.
I think I'll have a bite of the tasty Mars.
I am fed up, the stars are out again,
Wait! Wait! There's the flaming hot sun.
Thank goodness it's gone, I'm safe at last.

Laura Jane Rutter (9)
Pennington Junior School

COLOURS

Red is like blood dripping from a tap,
Blue is like the sky falling,
Green is like the long, tall grass,
Yellow is like the big, bright sun.

Red is like a shining apple,
Blue is like a dolphin jumping into the sea,
Green is like leaves falling from a tree,
Yellow is like daffodils coming through the ground.

Mikayla Warne (9)
Pennington Junior School

A COLOUR POEM

Purple is relaxing,
Purple is groovy:
Purple is peaceful,
Purple is light or dark:
Purple is interesting,
Purple is smooth:

Clear is see-through,
Clear you can see other colours:
Clear is gentle,
Clear is slippery:

Silver is shiny,
Silver is glittery:
Silver is eye-catching.

Natalie Marsh (9)
Pennington Junior School

SCHOOL

School is boring,
Some people say it's snazzy,
But I say it's rotten.
I work my socks off in maths,
I try to learn my 8 times table,
But I always fail.
Sometimes I get division right,
Sometimes I don't,
School is boring,
Don't say it is isn't!

Rosie Crumpton (9)
Pennington Junior School

Untitled

If gold was a person
Gold would look like
A ginger cat purring at the moonlit sky.
Gold would sound like a metal robot
Walking to school.
Gold would feel like a worn away key
Found at the king's palace.
Gold would smell like a warm cheese pasty
Cooking in the oven.

Arthur Chalk (8)
Pennington Junior School

Snap, Snap

As the alligators go snap, snap in the water
They swish their tails in and out of the water
They come out to play, alligators snap
They slide out of the night
And lay under the water
Like sleeping rocks, hard and grey rock.

Andrew Jones (8)
Pennington Junior School

Black

Black is like a burning rock,
Black is like a rotten egg,
Black is like a loud storm,
Black is like a man with a horn,
Black is like an oil can,
Black is like a monster.

Pierce Matthews (8)
Pennington Junior School

THE VOYAGE

Through the thick clouds,
Past the fresh breeze,
See the purple flowers,
Under the leafy trees.
Through the round bushes,
Under the sharp thorns,
See the green woodland,
Over the cut lawn.
Can you see the other world?
It's wonderland and there's a girl.
Now I had seen the lovely girl!
Time to travel to my own world.
I will travel far and wide.
I will be in disguise,
With symmetrical wings.
I'm now a butterfly.

Josie Lyne (9)
Pennington Junior School

MY FRIEND

My friend, Matthew
Is like a yummy roast dinner.
He makes me feel like a very, very nice dessert.
When we are together it is like a chocolate ice cream
And marshmallows.
When he is not with me I feel like a ship that has sunk.
What I like best about him is
When I have no one to play with he is there.

Lee Murray (8)
Pennington Junior School

COLOURS

Blue can be a dark colour
Blue can be a bright colour
Blue can be a disgusting colour
Blue can be a nice colour

Green is the colour of grass
Green glistens in the sun
Green is the colour of leaves in the spring
Green is a bright colour.

Stewart Humm (8)
Pennington Junior School

DESERT ISLANDS

Out in the desert, the hot sand sizzles
And the wind howls and whistles,
The palm trees sway,
In the warm breeze as I lay,
The waterfall plunges down and dances on the sparkling water,
As I lay drinking coconut milk.

Katherine Mapes (9)
Pennington Junior School

FAT CAT

One day I saw a fat cat
It wore a big old top hat
Next day I gave it a pat
And it scared off all the bats
Today it sat on our mat.

Amelia Sally Hamilton (9)
Pennington Junior School

A DANCING DOG

D ancing dog doing tap dancing
A unty dog doing the hula dance
N anny dog doing the cancan
C anadian dog doing the street dance
I ndian dog doing the river dance
N orthern Ireland dog doing a Scottish dance
G erman dog doing the Irish dance

D ogs all over the world dancing
O ther dogs lazing about in their houses
G oing to their baskets
S leeping while other dogs are dancing.

Robert Bailey (8)
Pennington Junior School

PEOPLE MAKE FUN OF MY FRECKLES

People make fun of my freckles,
They say that they look like big speckles.
But they think it is fun,
While I play in the sun.
I say there is nothing to laugh to,
But then I gave them a big clue.
I looked at one of them
And they looked like a speckled hen!
And he said, 'Oh what do I do?'
People make fun of my freckles,
They say they look like big speckles!

Sophie Louise House (9)
Pennington Junior School

SUNNY DAY

The sun is shining
We are at the beach
The silky sand slips through my toes and
                              covers my body
Every day I will go to this beach
Always the sun is shining
Tomorrow I will lie on that same beach
And a dog will come along
I will lift my hand in the air
He will start digging
He will stay for ages
My day will drift on
Warm, hot, sandy day.

Sian Bowen (8)
Pennington Junior School

MY LITTLE ISLAND

I once went on a voyage
My invisible friend and me,
To our little island floating on the sea,
A magical place where we can laugh
And always have some fun,
Under bright blue skies, lots of trees
And a big round blazing sun.
Fortunately my voyage back is a good voyage too,
For if I didn't have a voyage,
I couldn't write to you.

Jordan Baker (11)
Pennington Junior School

VOYAGE POEM

Looking at the shining rocket
Towering up above,
I climb upon the platform
To get to the cockpit.
The rocket entrance door opened
I carried on inside, I turned around and looked out
The ground was far below.
I pressed the entrance door button
The door slowly closed.

It wasn't long until we were in space,
I shut the engines down to land upon a planet
I pressed the entrance door button, the door slowly opened
I looked out, I saw a flashing light
I was scared.
I walked towards it, it was an alien!
I ran to my rocket, I stopped and looked again
He was nowhere to be seen.

I walked back into the rocket
I powered up the engines wanting to get home,
We saw the alien outside, so we threw him a bone,
It kept him very busy while we flew back home.
Suddenly I felt a bump!
I was back!
I jumped onto the platform, ran down the steps
I was glad to be back.
My family and friends were very happy
And we all lived in a big rocket-shaped house.

Rebecca Wallis (10)
Pennington Junior School

THERE WAS AN OLD MAN FROM LYMMINGTON

There was an old man from Lymmington
Who lost his old boot Wellington
He loved his boot
He gave a great shout
That weird old man from Lymmington.

Amy Broomfield (11)
Pennington Junior School

A POEM

A poem rhymes sometimes,
like Sally is my mother,
But Sonny is my brother.
My dad is very rarely sad
And other times very glad.

But other poems don't rhyme,
Like the flowers looked lovely
On the shelf!

Lily Winslow (7)
Pennington Junior School

MY FRIEND

My friend Stewart Humm
Is like a tub of ice cream
He makes me feel like a monkey with a banana
When we are together it is like a chocolate cake
When he is not with me it is like a blown-out fire
What I like best about him is he's a good football player.

Joe Baxter (8)
Pennington Junior School

MY DOGS

My dogs have
got coal-black noses
and sweet small faces.
One of them has a blonde
lightning bolt amongst
his black fur.
His name is Harry
after Harry Potter
because of his lightning bolt.
The other dog is called The Rock
because he always tries wrestling Harry.

Abbie Brownen (9)
Pennington Junior School

CATS AT HOME

C   ats sitting on the sofa
A   sleep in the cupboard
T   rying not to wreck the furniture
S   tealing food from the kitchen

A   lways smashing pottery
T   rying to eat our dinner

H   aving a poo on the stairs
O   n the plants and eating them
M   iaowing to get outside
E   ating all the time.

Adam Massarella (9)
Pennington Junior School

THE BLUE, BLUE SKY

B lue is the colour of a person sick
L adybirds fly in the deep blue sky
U nder the sea is a big white shark
E lephants are as naughty as me

S harks are as clever as me
K ites fly into the blue sky
Y achts sail across the seven seas.

Ryan James Brading (8)
Pennington Junior School

COLOUR POEM

Blue is fresh, clean, shiny
Blue is groovy, cool
Blue is calming, happy
Blue is eye-catching

Silver is glittery and shiny
Silver shimmers in the light
Silver is shiny, glitters in light
Silver sparkles like the sun.

Katie Louise McIntyre (9)
Pennington Junior School

ORANGE

Orange looks like the sun warming the frozen lake.
Orange feels like the skin of a fresh fruit.
Orange smells like a friendly fire on a cold Christmas night.
Orange tastes like fresh juice poured from a bottle.

Amy Clark (9)
Pennington Junior School

NIGHT

I met at dusk the knight of night,
A secretive, hard, tough bully,
As he appears comes a rumble of thunder,
As he departs comes a flash.

Wearing the cloak of a thousand storm clouds
And wearing the crown of stars,
The lightning cuffs make a very quick bang
Which the robe cannot cover.

On the other side of Heaven,
Is where the gloomy night lives,
The stars come to join him,
To cast his midnight shadows.

With the power of darkness to pour into the sky,
He kidnaps the light with the help from his stars,
He abandons his battle yet no one has won
He shuts the door on the light.

I am now hypnotised by night,
For he has the power and might,
He gives every small child a fright,
For he has the power and might.

Grace Spencer (10)
Queens Inclosure School

MY HAIR

Long hair
Short hair
Curly hair

Wavy hair
Brown hair
Blond hair

Everyone has different hair
Hair that is up
Hair that is not

Hair that is plaited
And tied in a knot.

Charlotte Pusey (8)
Queens Inclosure School

JUNGLE

Lots of menacing to do
I'm a good detective
I'll go and find a clue

I'm still walking
Monkeys are giggling
And I'm still walking
Alligators' tails are squiggling

I'm hiding in the leaves
Got my rucksack
I'm not in the countryside
With ponds with reeds

The insects are horrible
With big, ugly teeth
If you got bit by one
You'd be dead as a leaf

Now to catapult the bodies
They'd be dead as a net
For a long time
They won't see their pet.

Christopher Bond (8)
Queens Inclosure School

There's Something In The Garden Pond

There's something in the garden pond,
I wonder what it is?
There's something in the garden pond,
It's going to be swishing and gurgling next.

There's something in the garden pond,
It's bubbling and splashing now.
There's something in the garden pond,
It'll be fishing and diving next.
There's something in the garden pond,
It's as hungry as a shark.

There's something in the garden pond,
It's muddy, slimy and long.
There's something in the garden pond,
It's dirty, raggedy and slippery.
There's something in the garden pond,
It's mouldy, silly and stupid.
I can't think of anything else to say
So I'll just leave it there.

Zoe Hook (8)
Queens Inclosure School

The Deep Blue Sea

When I wake up in the morning I see the sea
I like to play near it and then it sees me
It twinkles in the bright light
It's loud when it's dark
And it is very quiet when it is sunny.

Georgia Preston (7)
Queens Inclosure School

NIGHT

A dark, gloomy night sweeps in on Monday
He was oversized, ugly and black.
He had a black cloak of a thousand storm clouds.
Tough and strong witch made me scared,
Cold and alone, shivering like mad.
On the peak of the tall mountain
Lived the oversized, ugly and black night.
Night kidnaps light and abandons him,
Leaving people in bed asleep.

Night looked so ugly and he needed a makeover,
I was so scared, I could not move a bit.

Natasha Longland (10)
Queens Inclosure School

THE DEEP BLUE RIVER

The deep blue river is a meandering path,
A glistening river as calm as the grass,
As deep as a metre going fast, fast, fast.
The river whistles like the wind,
A deep blue river looks really nice,
In a bright moonlit sky.
The deep blue river gets really fierce,
It growls like a lion,
It is as long as iron.
The deep blue river steals precious stuff,
It keeps them forever,
It's really tough.

Matthew Jenner (8)
Queens Inclosure School

THE COLOURFUL RAINBOW

Here is the bight light that opens your eyes,
See the colours that light up,
Look at the dazzling pound,
See the petals fall,
Smell the lovely scented flowers,
See the long green grass that's flowing in the air,
Smell the cooking that's going on over there.

Felicity Shand (8)
Queens Inclosure School

AUTUMN

A   utumn is a time when the leaves come off the trees
U   nder the sky the trees are bare
T   he trees are bare and dying
U   nder the ground the badgers, moles and rabbits are digging
M   ummies and daddies are getting the children back inside
N   o one's outside, but everyone's inside.

Curtis Murphy (8)
Queens Inclosure School

UP IN HEAVEN

Up in Heaven fairies play the harp
Picking apples on the tree
Practicing dancing in the sunlight
Pretty dresses shining bright
Shining brightly like the sun
And singing good like God.

Charlotte Roberts (8)
Queens Inclosure School

THE SEA

My big sister said to me,
'We're in the water, can't you see?
Now please don't throw pebbles at me.
The sea is so beautiful, the sea is so beautiful,
The sea is so green.
We're in the water, can't you see?
Now please don't be silly and laugh at me.
We're in the water, can't you see?
Now please don't be stupid and buzz like a bee.
The sea is so glittery and blue and green.
I've told you not to be silly!'

Elena Tsibouklis (8)
Queens Inclosure School

BODY

Your body is fat
Your body is large
Your body is greedy
Your body is large
Your body is thin
Your body is tall
Your body can sometimes be very small

But best of all your body isn't tall
Or small or fat or thin
No, it is *enormous!*

Sarah Hulme (8)
Queens Inclosure School

HEAVEN

Countryside, wonderful countryside, hills, wonderful hills, streams with
lilies, wonderful streams with lilies.
Roses, wonderful roses, poppies, wonderful poppies, daisies, wonderful
daisies, bluebells, wonderful bluebells.
Palm trees, wonderful palm trees, willow trees, wonderful willow trees,
blossom trees, wonderful blossom trees.
Dolphins, wonderful dolphins, whales, wonderful whales, starfish,
wonderful starfish, foxes, wonderful foxes, badgers, wonderful badgers.
Rabbits, wonderful rabbits, sunshine, wonderful sunshine, gorgeous
sunsets, wonderful sunsets, funfairs, wonderful funfairs, circuses,
wonderful circuses, friendship, wonderful friendship, birds,
wonderful birds.
Waterfalls, wonderful waterfalls.

Imogen Clarke (8)
Queens Inclosure School

CATERPILLAR

Oh Mr Caterpillar
How slow and steady you go.
How soft and hairy you are.
Mrs Bird is hovering
Saying, 'Today's the day
You'll be so beautiful!'
Oh Mr Caterpillar
Closing up to a leaf
When suddenly you turn into a
. . . Butterfly!

Elicia McGregor (8)
Queens Inclosure School

INSECTS

Insects are small
Insects are big
Insects are speedy
Insects are dense
Insects sometimes are yucky
Insects sting
Insects sometimes don't sting
And these are *insects*.

Dipen Pandya (8)
Queens Inclosure School

LIMERICK!

There was a young man called Murray
Who liked eating very hot curry.
He once hit his head
And now he is dead
So he said bye bye to Surrey.

Connal Dyke (10)
Romsey Junior School

LIMERICK

There was a young man from Brazil,
Who always ate his fill,
One day he cursed
And so was burst,
By a man on the top of a hill.

James Perry (10)
Romsey Junior School

FISH

He swims through streams
as he dreams . . .
at this point
he found a wing joint!

He ate it for dinner
not getting thinner
as he was looking
the fishermen were hooking!

One soon caught him
as he was dim
and that poor small fish
ended up a great dish.

Neal Reeves (10)
Romsey Junior School

THE SILVER BIRCH

He is lonely standing on his own,
he needs someone to speak to.

He is cold as the wind blows softly.

He doesn't like children
swinging on the branch.
Pulling the bark off.

When the snow falls,
people break sticks off me.

Sometimes I'm scared that I will die.

Daniel Cook (11)
Romsey Junior School

A MOTHER'S POINT OF VIEW

When you're in a noisy plane
it's hard to keep your children tame
and when a dress you're trying to pick,
the little ones are always sick.
When you're doing the washing up,
they say the computer's all jammed up.
But when you take them all to school,
you find you're lonely after all!

Caitlin Monahan (9)
Romsey Junior School

I LOVE

I love food and drink
I love my family
Why is there love?
I love the gold sun
I love to play
Why is there love?
I love dogs
I love cats
Why is there love
I love English
I love football
Just why is there love?
I love to write neat
I love to go to the shop
Love helps you get better at things
I just love the world!

Louisa Castle (7)
Romsey Junior School

WINTER

Winter is like a snow king,
The world is his kingdom,
He hates all living things,
Especially the other kings.

He loves to fight battles,
Because every time he wins,
He has an army of snowflakes,
As strong as a thousand men.

Spring is his worst enemy,
He has an army of blossom,
They're also as strong as a thousand men.

One day they came head-to-head on a field,
Only one can leave triumphant.

Spring seized the king and locked him in a dungeon,
Only to be freed,
After autumn has gone.

Thomas Humphreys (10)
Romsey Junior School

A MONSTER TREE

Standing there in front of me,
A grizzly, green tree.
He's reaching out his hand,
Its roots - like stringy rubber bands.
Winter's tree is tall and bare,
Summer comes, it now has hair.
Autumn leaves turn orange, yellow, red,
It seems to say, go to bed.

Clare Neale (10)
Romsey Junior School

GIRLS

I'm going to jump on my bed Mum
Don't!
Too late!
Well stop it now!

It's the end of the day
Well go to sleep then
No, I'm going to the pub!

Next morning
Bish! Bash! Bong!
Mum! Hannah just gave me a black eye
Hannah stop it this instant!

Mum, I've made my bed
Well, what's that you said?
I've made my bed
That's great!

Tess Phippen (7)
Romsey Junior School

WINTER IS A PRACTICAL JOKER

Winter is a practical joker
Making everywhere as white as a polar bear
Winter is a practical joker
Blocking up lots of doorways
Winter is a practical joker
Making someone slip upon the ice
Winter is a practical joker
Trapping people in his avalanches
Winter is a practical joker
Throwing snowballs at everyone.

Jason King (10)
Romsey Junior School

THE OLD TREE

I'm old and I am wrinkled
I've not always been this way
I used to bloom with blossom
- But now I only sway.

It's always just like winter
When I am dark and bare
Now, it's always like that,
- Oh dear; it's just not fair.

I used to entertain
With all my marvellous shows
But now I am retired,
- And I will never grow.

I used to be quite pretty
I was red, gold and green
Now, I'm black and withered,
- I'm not like I used to be.

I wish I wasn't old
It's something I don't want to be
But it's the truth, let's face it
- I'll always be a tree.

Helen Le Grice (10)
Romsey Junior School

A TREE FROM THE PAST

Big and strong
Lived for long
Tall and high
Reaching for the sky

Imagine what the tree could tell
Living through rain, snow, wind and hail
Telling tales from the past
Short stories that will forever last.

Kelly Blackmore (11)
Romsey Junior School

THE MIX-UP TREE

On the tree green leaves
green leaves on the tree
the red and green apples
we eat for our supper and tea.

Children throwing sticks
to knock the conkers down
then falling, falling, falling
right to the very ground.

I felt a sudden breeze
when I looked up at the tree
it was reaching for my hand
when it looked back down at me.

The tree is big to me
although I am a creature
the light and dark leaves
has a lot of feature.

I wake up in the morning
the tree then sets me free
I go to sleep at dark
the tree is there for me.

Leanne Edwards (10)
Romsey Junior School

I LOVE . . .

I love my mummy because she gives me big sloppy kisses
and warm cuddly hugs.
Isn't love great!
I love my dad because he carries me up the stairs to bed.
Isn't love great!
I love my sister because she has lots of cool stuff.
Isn't love great!
I love my rabbit called Mascara because she's cute and furry.
Isn't love great!
I love my cousins because they play fun games.
Isn't love great!
I love my bed because it's hot and cosy.
Isn't love great!

Leanne Wheeler (8)
Romsey Junior School

LIFE OUT OF DEATH

I used to be a magnificent, strong tree,
But now I am rotting - just falling debris,
Before I died, I planted my final seed,
When it first sprouted, a little, green weed,
All flimsy, a sapling - like I used to be.
His leaves youthful, unlike mine which are crinkling,
He became stronger, his bark started wrinkling,
His branches forked like lightning; I'm proud he is mine,
Towering above me, most handsome and fine,
As he peered at the heap that used to be me.

Francesca Hughes (11)
Romsey Junior School

A TREE

Trees are somewhere
where you can
go to think.

Trees are somewhere
where you can
cool down.

Trees are somewhere
where you can
think of your loved ones.

Trees are somewhere
where you can
go if you are feeling sad.

Trees are somewhere
where you can
look up at someone
if you want them to forgive you.

Georgina Day (11)
Romsey Junior School

TREES

Trees live forever
Not like us, we come and go.
Swaying slowly, side to side.
A gentle breeze, she blows.
Great, thick branches
Reaching for the sky.
Unless people destroy them,
It'll be a long time till they say goodbye.

Sian Holloway (11)
Romsey Junior School

TREES

Trees big and bold.
Trees tall and small.
Some bright as gold.
Some dark as night.
Every year, new leaves.
Everywhere you look.
Right, left, forward, behind,
Trees live
Longer than people.
Trees.

Brett Ricketts (11)
Romsey Junior School

THE WEATHER MAN

The weather man is never true,
He gets ideas while visiting the loo,
Every year he gets sacked,
But every year he comes back,
He always tries to be the best,
But he never qualified in a test,
To be a weather man!

Cameron Messenger (8)
Romsey Junior School

BLUE

The glow of love in a cold dark corner
Icy cold fingers standing still
The icy cold sea crashing against the shore
The clear sky shining on the gloomy sea.

Dalton Malone (8)
Romsey Junior School

ROUND OUR WAY

At number one
Is Mr Chunn
Who always thinks of fun.

At number two
There's Bertie Blue
Who always says 'Achoo'.

At number three
Well, that's just me
And I'll be in today.

At number four
There are the Bores
Who love to do encores!

At number five
Old Mrs Slice
Who often gives us pies.

And that's our way
I hope it's clear
Take it or leave it
Cos we'll be here!

Claire Anderson (11)
Romsey Junior School

YELLOW

The gleam of the beautiful golden sun,
When the daffodils shin below.
When I'm pale, I feel sad.
The buttercups sway beneath the yellow sun.
The golden fire is burning in the forest.

Samantha Hawton (7)
Romsey Junior School

A REBELLIOUS TEENAGER

A teenager is like dark, cold nights at winter.
Blows leaves off the trees with temper.
She turns up the leaves when she spins around and around.
When she's in a mood, she stamps;
Freezing trees, ponds and grass.
When she cries in pain, the winter winds howl.
The sky is filled with grey clouds with her hurt.
When she is alone and quiet she makes glittery
White snowflakes fall down softly
Making her life a lot happier with glowing peace.

Nicole Sparham (11)
Romsey Junior School

HUNGRY IN THE NIGHT

I crept out of bed,
I put my dressing gown on.
Then I opened my door silently.
I crept down the staircase going onto the kitchen floorboards.
I opened the fridge door to eat the last bit of chocolate cake.
I left the fridge open to see what happened in the morning.
Then I crept out of the kitchen and crept upstairs and slipped
into bed.
When I woke up in the morning some things were melted
And some things were warm.
I do the same every night!

Ashleigh Cardy (7)
Romsey Junior School

HUNGRY IN THE NIGHT

I stirred,
I heard my tummy rumbling,
I suddenly decided to go downstairs
And eat the last of the chocolate cake.
I crept out of bed,
I froze!
I saw my mum come out of her bedroom.
I stood there shivering,
My mum saw me and put me to bed again.
She was really angry with me.
I took a deep breath,
I started to get out of bed again.
This time I had luck,
I reached the stairs and crept down them.
I tiptoed round the creaky floorboard.
I went to the kitchen door,
I opened the fridge door and found no chocolate cake.
I went back to bed walking over the creaky floorboard as I went.
Mum shouted 'Get back to bed! But if you're looking
For the chocolate cake I ate it!'

Amber Tesch (7)
Romsey Junior School

WHY?

Why am I eight? I hate it!
I'm not allowed to do anything!
Why did I see a mayor sitting in a chair?
Why aren't I allowed at the park?
Why have you got a son called Mark?
Why is my brother allowed a PC?
Why am I not allowed to scream?

Megan Moore (7)
Romsey Junior School

SHINING

In the night a colour is shining at me,
What is it?
Is it a colour or isn't it?
I don't know.
Let's go and see
That thing shining at me!

Oliver Le Peuple (8)
Romsey Junior School

WEEKDAY WEATHER

On Monday rain covers the world just like the click of two fingers;
Tuesday, rain drizzles like a tap dripping water into a china cup;
On Wednesday, a fog, like steam coming from an oven fills the air;
Thursday, a roaring wind sweeps the land like a dolphin jumping
from the sea;
On Friday the furious wind calms down to a light breeze;
Saturday, the sun pops out bright and warm as could be;
On Sunday the beautiful golden sun burns people so they suffer
singeing skin.

Alex Lee (8)
Romsey Junior School

YELLOW

Lightning strikes with
the moonlight and the stars
shining on the land, the sun
rising, stopping the lightning
happening, sunflowers rising
from the blackness.

Max Beale (7)
Romsey Junior School

Instructions For Opening Your Presents

1) First get to the tree and grab your present,
2) Elbow your brother out of the way.
3) Open your present as fast as you can and don't bother to look who it is from.
4) Open your box with the present in.
5) Then play with your new toy excitedly for three minutes.
6) Then smile at the person who gave you your present.
Repeat numbers 1-6 again.

Liam Holt (8)
Romsey Junior School

My Cat

When my cat wakes up, he's very silky.
Then I get a piece of string,
He chases it like the string is a snake and he is a lion.
Then he jumps on me and starts licking me on the face.
I chase him down the stairs then he chases me.
He rushes to the cat flap then he goes out and plays in the bushes.
Finally he come in and goes to sleep on my bed all curled up.

Natalie Felton (7)
Romsey Junior School

Green

Grass growing out in the fields,
Eyes show us our feelings.
Trees swaying in the breeze.
The sea needs its sea creatures.
An emerald shining in the sun.

Sarah Mingay (8)
Romsey Junior School

WHY AND WHAT

Come on let's go to your nice warm bed.
Why?
Because it's bedtime.
Why?
Oh! Come on it's bedtime . . . I'll tell you a new story.
Why?

Wake up . . . sleepy head!
Why?
Oh! *Not again!*
What?
We are late, come on we are going Twyford to get you a new computer.
Why?
They have got computers there, you can do ICT.
Why?
You need a new computer.
Why?
Because yours has broken down.
Why?
Stop saying why? . . . Why? . . . Why?
Why Mummy?

Helen Goodyear (7)
Romsey Junior School

YELLOW

The sun shining its beautiful light.
Eating bananas.
The stars glinting at night.
Daisies reaching for the sun.

Samantha Peris-Perez (8)
Romsey Junior School

USELESS

As useless as a cheater who plays fair,
As useless as a lady with no hair.
As useless as a stage with no floor.
As useless as a room with no door.

As useless as a cat with no paws,
As useless as a bear with no claws.
As useless as a spider with no legs,
As useless as a washing line with no pegs.

As useless as a keyboard with no keys,
As useless as a beehive with no bees.
As useless as a clock with no hands,
As useless as a world with no land.

As useless as a rabbit with no ears,
As useless as a pub with no beers.
As useless as a clown that's not funny,
As useless as treacle that's not runny.

As useless as a book with no pages,
As useless as a zoo with no cages.
As useless as a person with no brain,
As useless as a street with no name.

Luke Barrett (9)
Romsey Junior School

BLACK

Night-time sleep
The thunderstorm crashing through the sky
Rain making me in a bad mood
My trousers as dark as the chalkboard.

Ben Nachman (8)
Romsey Junior School

WEEKLY WEATHER

My week went like this:
On Monday I happily played in the golden sun.
On Tuesday it was wet and windy.
On Wednesday it was horrible and foggy so I did a puzzle.
On Thursday it was tipping down with rain so I slept all day.
On Friday the wind ripped my gown off the line.
On Saturday I caught a cold.
On Sunday the sun suddenly sprang up.

Sophie Sadler (8)
Romsey Junior School

THE WEATHER IS . . .

The rain pours down like houses,
We call it 'raining cats and dogs',
The ground is wet and muddy,
It is like a colossal bog.

'Blame that weather man mate,'
We say 'We want blue sky!;
Blue sky, blue sky, we want blue sky!
What's happening? The sky's turning blue,
Hurray!

Joel Kirkland (7)
Romsey Junior School

WHITE

Clouds floating around in the sky,
The glow of the fairy brightening everything.
Frost trickling off a tree onto me,
Pages of a book flickering, no writing at all.

The moon shining down on us,
Silence on a misty day,
Fear on a person's face,
One side of a chessboard.

Hazel Townsend (7)
Romsey Junior School

WHAT IS A MILLION

The branches of a forest.
The petals on a daisy are blowing in the wind.
The people's names in the world.
The planets up in the sky.
The grass blowing in the wind.
The books that you read so much.
The food in the world is tasty.
The crashing waves in the sea.

Nicolle Shuter (8)
Romsey Junior School

THE LIFE OF A SHOE

I have felt many times
the same feet of my friend.
They have tickled me often,
but now I am worn and torn
and my toes are ripped.
I'm in the dump,
I'm dying!

Megan Tarrant (7)
Romsey Junior School

BLUE!

The colour of the berries you eat.
A kentrosaurus roaring at you.
A quartz crystal shining in your face.
A water springtail wriggling in the river.
The dolphin splashing in the sea.
The colour of eyes watching you.
A butterfly fluttering around.

Fay Clare (8)
Romsey Junior School

RED

Blood pumping through veins
the dragon breathing fire
tomato being squashed
pin being squashed into the wall
poppies being picked
book opening
pen being thrown away
a door opening.

Nathan Tizard (7)
Romsey Junior School

BLUE

Blue is the colour of a flower.
Blue is the sign for cold.
Blue sea as well.
Blue is for a whale too.

Alice Roud (7)
Romsey Junior School

WHITE

The clouds surrounding you.
Your glittering teeth.
Very, very quiet.
The look on your face when you're ill.
The outside of your eyeball.
The paper flying around.
The normal colour.

Matthew Garner (8)
Romsey Junior School

RED

Poppies telling us how many people died in the armies.
The heat pumping up and down.
Juicy grapes that are sweet.
The hotness of fire spreading.
Lipstick staining dry lips.

Georgina Barnes (8)
Romsey Junior School

RED

Tomato soup and bread.
Sitting by a warm fire.
Dreaming of strawberry pie for pudding
With shiny apples beside.

Manney Vane (7)
Romsey Junior School

FLOODS

It's a freezing cold day in January mist,
As Dad filled the fire the flame licked and hissed,
Then bang! Crash! Wallop! The rain hit the house,
The pots and pans fell and just missed a mouse.
A flowing stream crept right under the door
And ruined Mum's carpet on the living room floor.
Now the water level is rising up quickly,
We have to leave the cat with Uncle Quigly.
I'm sitting in our old boat with its broken mast,
'Hurry up,' complained Tom, 'we need to move fast.'
We arrived at the shelter, it's ever so boring,
We have to stay here until it's morning.
The floods are over, the damage is done,
I don't want another because they are not much fun.

Samantha Allan (10)
St Peter's Catholic Primary School, Waterlooville

THIS IS ME IN MY DREAMS

I would see the birds fluttering in the trees,
Mice darting into dark corners,
I would feel the wind blowing through my fur,
Hear car revving, motorbikes roaring,
People working, taste my treats.

This is me . . . the cat.

Danni Avery (9)
St Peter's Catholic Primary School, Waterlooville

WHY?

Why do floods happen?
Why do wars start?
People have no homes,
What's the point in that?
People get killed, why?
I ask myself.
I feel sad, why?
To see all this.

On the TV,
In the paper,
See many tragedies,
Killing and fighting,
When people die.
I feel sad, why?
To see all this
Killing and fighting.

Why? Why? Why? Why? *Why?*

Emma Wray (10)
St Peter's Catholic Primary School, Waterlooville

THIS IS ME IN MY DREAMS

In my dreams I want to be in the army.
In the army I could feel a gun, the gun feels heavy and hot.
I can see many guns, I can hear shouting by men dying
And gunfire and can smell smoke from the guns . . .

Neil Baxter (10)
St Peter's Catholic Primary School, Waterlooville

SCHOOL

In a wonderfully colourful classroom,
Jane was working on a maths sum till noon,
The teacher said, 'Too much noise everyone.'
Then the clouds went and covered the bright sun,
The bell rang to signal the end of class,
When suddenly someone broke a small glass.
Mrs Land said, 'Time to go out to play.'
But everyone moaned, 'Oh! Not today.'

Except for Jane who wanted to go,
For laying outside was the fresh crisp snow.
So Jane and her friends went out to play tag,
Though all of the young girls really did nag.
Then the teacher rang a little old bell,
They went back inside and Jane said, 'Oh well!'

Kirsty Markham (9)
St Peter's Catholic Primary School, Waterlooville

SID

Once there was a boy whose name was Sid
He lived in a place called Madrid
One day he had to move far away
So he ran up to his bed and lay
He squeezed into his bedroom cupboard
He cuddled his teddy Mr Hubourd
But after a while he starved to death
He ran downstairs and lost his breath

At the bottom to his surprise
His mum and dad narrowed their eyes
They forced him into the old car
He was given a chocolate bar
He leapt from the car, hurting his knees
He had to move despite his pleas.

Aiden Yates (9)
St Peter's Catholic Primary School, Waterlooville

SNOW

Snowflakes falling from the air,
Looking at it lying there.
People watching in a trance,
Trying to have a little glance.
Gliding down upon the trees,
Blowing and floating in the breeze.
Whirling and swirling all around,
Eventually landing on the ground.

Children running, shouting, cheering,
Cars are sliding, brakes are screaming.
Sledding, skiing, down the run,
Everybody having fun.
Building snowmen such a task,
See you in the morning, hope you last!

Stephanie Bone (10)
St Peter's Catholic Primary School, Waterlooville

THE SEASON OF LIFE

Pause for one moment, consider with me,
The beauty of nature before our eyes,
All the wondrous sights, which we can see,
Seeds of life mysteriously arise.
The sweet scented jasmine, bursts into bud,
The pansies and primroses shyly peep,
Frogs jump in puddles and frolic in mud
And creatures awake from their winter's sleep.
From cocoons emerge each new butterfly,
Lilac and yellow and scarlet and blue,
The skylarks and nightingales flutter by,
Joyfully singing, they fly out of view.
This vision appears beyond the hill's crest,
During springtime, may all creatures be blessed.

Clare Harris (10)
St Peter's Catholic Primary School, Waterlooville

HOW LOVELY

A glimmer of sunshine
that fell on her cheek,
her eyes turned to sapphires
her hair turned to gold.
The warm breeze in the trees
and the dewdrops on flowers
her hair bound by dewdrops
her ring was a flower.

It sat by her gentle
it twisted and turned
a rose grew beside her
how lovely
how lovely they murmured
all in a hush and a whisper.

Siobhán Ward-Farrell (10)
St Peter's Catholic Primary School, Waterlooville

THE MEADOW

The wind blew through the long, tall grass
And set the flowers whispering.
The daisy said to the poppy,
'I wish I was tall like you!'
But the poppy said, 'No you're small and neat,
Just like the clover who smells so sweet!'
The clover looked up at the buttercup
And wished that she was yellow.

This went on all day, until,
A blue-eyed girl skipped down the hill,
And bending down she picked the flowers,
And said, 'I've been searching for you for hours,
You look so pretty when you are together.'
And then the flowers all smiled with pleasure.

Rebecca Rimmer (9)
St Peter's Catholic Primary School, Waterlooville

PEEK INTO PARADISE

The sand, silver on the deserted beach,
Like fresh alpine snow,
The calm millpond sea contemplates its next moon-planned journey;
White foals leap gleefully in their cool, blue pen.

Crowned palms sway to the breeze's sweet melody, proudly
Bowing and curtseying,
In the humid night-time air.
Their young seedlings are nourished with its sweet song.
Doves perch on broad branches, cooing.
Monkeys toss exotic fruits.
Fish swim joyfully in their own forest of coral.
Sunset . . . changing the blazing sun to a feeble, dimly glowing ember,
Editing the fabric of time.
The only inhabitants on the beach are the solemn expressionless rocks,
Grand palaces of the island.
No footprints in the sand,
Calm serenity.
An island floating in the clouds.
Paradise.

Martin Thompson (10)
St Peter's Catholic Primary School, Waterlooville

THE BOOMING STORM

I saw the clouds gather,
I heard the drizzling rain.
The thunder started booming,
The storm had begun.

Olivia Stirman (10)
St Peter's Catholic Primary School, Waterlooville

A Day Of Sea

Gentle waves, in the early morning sunlight -
Mindlessly drifting in the feeble breeze -
Reflect a sapphire-blue sky,
With clouds fringed with foam of diamond lace.

The waves grow stronger with the sunlight.
A swirling torrent of icy waters
Disputes with the golden sands,
About who is rightful king.

After the storm, the sea is tranquil and quiet.
Only a ripple can be seen,
On these lone and deserted waters.
The desolate sands lie all forlorn,
In mountainous heaps,
Where the sea so ruthlessly placed them,
In that sudden fit of rage.

As the sun prepares to slumber,
And the eerie silver moonlight
Takes its throne of glory,
The sea is fully calm.
The waters are a sheet of glass,
Unveiling all the secrets -
Of how - and why - this change takes place;
And when this glass transforms to fire,
Sunset has fallen on the Earth.

Yet no one will ever visit this ocean of change.
For as each day goes on and on,
And as the years go by,
This beach will always remain the same,
Because I see it -
I see it with my mind's eye.

Rebecca Ryan (10)
St Peter's Catholic Primary School, Waterlooville

MY LOUNGE FIRE

My lounge fire,
Surrounded by red bricks,
Hot, blazing, roaring.
Flickering like a torch,
Running out of batteries,
Hot like the sun in summer.
It makes me feel at peace,
Warm like being wrapped
In a cosy blanket.
My lounge fire
Makes me think of people
Sleeping on the streets.

Richard Evans (10)
St Peter's RC Primary School, Winchester

THE CRYING WIND

Sometimes can e calm
sometimes fierce
gentle, raging, howling.
Howling like a hungry wolf,
gentle as a touch of silk,
it makes me feel cold -
As cold as a frosty winter's morning.
The crying wind
reminds us how life changes
from day to day.

Helen Oliver (10)
St Peter's RC Primary School, Winchester

THE KITCHEN TABLE

The kitchen table is a spy,
always listening to every conversation.
Father's moans, mother's rants, children's squabbles,
making notes at every hesitation.

Trials and tribulations of being a table:
Its back all a mess, with spilt food telling its fable.
Pencils from a human's letter digging in,
Hot plates I can't even imagine.

Best of friends are the chairs,
Enduring their shares.
Sat on three times a day,
Often in an uncomfy way.

Alex Dean (10)
St Peter's RC Primary School, Winchester

THE RIVER ITCHEN

The River Itchen,
Through the meadow at St Cross,
Wide, smooth, calm,
Like a shiny snake slithering through the undergrowth;
Like the clouds sailing by.
It relaxes me,
Like the day floating past me before I fall asleep.
The River Itchen
Helps me see what's important.

Ruth McElroy (10)
St Peter's RC Primary School, Winchester

THE WIND

The wind is all around me
When will it ever start?
Swirling and swizzling
Until the rain clouds part.

The northern wind is howling
Like a wolf in the moonlight
All the animals wide awake
And lots of them in fright.

Rampaging and destructive
When will it ever stop?
The wind is all around me
When will it ever stop?

Patrick Miles (10)
St Peter's RC Primary School, Winchester

SPACE

Space.
Where no man has been before.
An empty, swirling vacuum.
Black, like the darkest night of all,
Like a never-ending story,
Always waiting to be explored.
It makes me feel insignificant,
Like a single star in the night sky.
Space.
As old as God himself.

Stanley Sawyer (10)
St Peter's RC Primary School, Winchester

THE WIND

The wind is a wolf,
He is lively and boisterous in spring,
He is calm and gentle in the summer
And that is when he mostly sleeps.
He uses the sky as his rug and the earth as his basket.

In the autumn he shakes leaves from trees
And makes them fall gently to the ground.
He sends the birds to warmer climates.
He licks a face with his icy cold tongue.
He runs like a cheetah, air streaming behind him.
He sometimes creates a hurricane.

He nips at a cheek on a winter's day,
He swims in the sea and makes it stormy.
He howls mournfully,
Sometimes he's angry, raging and is life-threatening.

We can sometimes hear him, often feel him, never see him,
But we know he's there - raging or peaceful in all seasons.

Nick Sharpe (10)
St Peter's RC Primary School, Winchester

THE OCEAN

The ocean,
Destructive, raging, menacing,
A home to sea creatures,
Like a huge giant, stamping fiercely,
It makes me feel weak, like a tiny mouse,
The ocean,
A monster to some, but good to others.

Annemarie Smith (10)
St Peter's RC Primary School, Winchester

THE STORM

Rainy ruin,
    Windy weekend,
        Building blower,
    Monday mourner,
Lake leaker,
    Wave waker,
        Terrifying torment,
    Hedge hinderer,
Tree toppler,
    Bush beater,
        Wet waltzer,
    Gaiting gale,
Car consumer!

Oliver Taylor (11)
St Peter's RC Primary School, Winchester

THE PERFECT STORM

The perfect storm,
Makes huge waves and rattles windows.
Dangerous, deadly, destructive.
Like a perfected piece of art,
Like an earthquake.
It makes me feel worried and scared,
It's like I'm being ignored.
The perfect storm,
It makes me think the world is going to end.

Declan Hart (11)
St Peter's RC Primary School, Winchester

THE BEST MONTHS

August, bringing last of sun,
Soon back to school,
The end of fun.

September, it's very bad,
The end of the holidays,
I'm very sad.

October, blustery showers,
Things are dying,
End of flowers.

November, Bonfire Night is here,
Winter has arrived,
The nights are cold and clear.

Now we have December,
Christmas is nearly here,
For everyone to remember.

Theresa Woodford (10)
St Peter's RC Primary School, Winchester

THE WIND

The wind
Is part of nature
Strong, gusty and cold
Like a giant breathing
Like a ghost howling
It makes me feel wild
Like a dog chasing its tail
The wind
Makes me feel powerless.

Claudia Hindle (9)
St Peter's RC Primary School, Winchester

CAT KENNING

My cat is a
    nine lifer
    loveable licker
    rat ripper
    miaow maker
    tail swisher
    sneaky fisher
    angry scratcher
    milk manic
    fluffy killer
    whisker twitcher
    tree climber
    warm welcomer
    secret hider.
That's my cat!

Mairead O'Kelly (9)
St Peter's RC Primary School, Winchester

THE STORM

The storm,
Destroys anything which stands in its way,
Swirling, whirling, destructive,
Like a dinosaur hunting,
Like a lion cautiously roaming the grasslands,
I feel like a helpless little mouse ready to be attacked,
The storm,
I think it is like a mouse being hunted by a cat,
But we are the mice and the storm is the cat.

Robert Pettigrew (11)
St Peter's RC Primary School, Winchester

CATS

Midnight howler
Prancing prowler

Mouse masher
Bird basher

Water hater
Fish baiter

Leather cushion paws
Sharp shiny claws

Black, white or tabby
Smart groomed or shabby

Long tail, short tail or Manx
They're sure to get up to some pranks.

Gregory Kidd (9)
St Peter's RC Primary School, Winchester

THE PLANE

A plane easing through the sky
Swiftly moving through the clouds
Dipping and diving through the air
Bang
Falling like a shooting star
Just dust to the ocean
Water seeping through the window
Up, up through the air in just your seat

Nothingness, starving, thirsty until . . .

Felix Jarrey (10)
St Peter's RC Primary School, Winchester

STORM

The ghostly storm
Howling and screaming
It streaks past your eyes
Scratching and slashing at whoever it flies by
It draws an ice cold rattling breath
Blowing through the day and well into the night
And then soundly it sleeps
No one knowing it's there
Hiding in the sea
Quietly mourning, whimpering sorrowfully
And again its temper's high
It's in a rage and is blowing sky high
Banging on your door saying: 'Let me in!'
Anger its fuel, it rages on
I'm in such a frenzy, I'll swirl you up whole
Watch out, guess who?
I'm your worst nightmare and I'm right after you
Brick walls and fences are no match for me
The USA army are just like dumplings in the sea
Revenge will be mine for you think the 'rocks' tough
Well, what am I?
Dangerous
Devastating
Ferocious and free
Angry and ghostly
A haunting nightmare teasing you wilfully
Torturing my prey.

Marcus Martin (10)
St Peter's RC Primary School, Winchester

THE OLD OAK

The old oak,
The father of time,
As old as the world,
As wise as an owl,
Proudly displaying
His leafy plumage
Like a proud peacock.

The old oak,
The mysterious watcher,
As silent as ever,
As the seasons weather him,
There he stands,
Gnarled and bent,
Boughing to strangers,
Like a statue he stands.

The old oak,
The king of the meadow,
As a ruler above all.
As centuries roll by,
It's just another second,
In the life of the oak,
He still lives on.

The old oak,
The great and majestic,
As the men approach,
As they carry their saws,
Coming to seek him.
But before he goes,
He sheds some acorns,
His successors to be.

Edward Alveyn (10)
St Peter's RC Primary School, Winchester

THE DAY OF THE CAT

Early waker
People shaker

Loveable licker
Rat ripper

Bird slayer
Human scratcher

Fluffy snuggler
Naughty twitcher

Lazy sleeper
Curtain scratcher

Mouse masher
Sneaky killer

Evening curler
Midnight howler.

Jamie Birchall (10)
St Peter's RC Primary School, Winchester

THE SEA

I am a bath tub,
A place to have fun,
Lots of children visit,
But everybody can come.

My shores are for castles,
That are made out of sand,
But when a machine comes,
They spoil the whole land!

Charlotte Martin (9)
St Peter's RC Primary School, Winchester

MY CAT

Bird slayer,
Sneaky killer,
Rat ripper,
Sneaky food eater,
Dog scratcher,
Broomstick rider.

Ian Hadaway (9)
St Peter's RC Primary School, Winchester

THE WIND

A hat-stealer
  A window-rattler

    A dress-dryer
    A frock-flier

      A flag-flutterer
        A truck-turnoverer.

Natasha Dean (10)
St Peter's RC Primary School, Winchester

THE LION

Prowling, crawling, seeking,
The lion creeps through the long, fresh grass,
Hunting for its prey,
The lion is its own thunderstorm,
It is the sun, striding across the sky,
It is a planet, going round in circles.
The lion,
A magnificent creature, the king of the jungle.

Sarah Morgan (10)
St Peter's RC Primary School, Winchester

OUR ENORMOUS GALAXY

Our enormous galaxy,
Known as the Milky Way,
Humongous, amazing, colourful,
Like a sparkling tiara,
Like the background for a picture;
It makes me feel tiny,
Like a speck of dust;
Our enormous galaxy,
Shows us how big things can be!

Kathryn Heneghan (10)
St Peter's RC Primary School, Winchester

THE WIND

The wind
Nips at my cheek when it blows.
Teasing, tickling, tapping,
Like a wolf weeping,
Like a fish's tail wavering.
It makes me feel swished about.
Makes me feel like the only victim.
The wind
Reminds us how powerful nature is.

Alanna Nouwens (9)
St Peter's RC Primary School, Winchester

THE WIND

As he swifts past the window
looking with an eager smile

Although we cannot see him
he'll float from mile to mile

As he shakes trees so viciously
you get shivers down your spine

He'll then be satisfied with his work
and leave a dreadful mine!

Emily Bell (10)
St Peter's RC Primary School, Winchester

DINNER DISASTER

I sat down in such a state,
I accidentally ate my plate.

I left my peas, I left my beans
And spilt the gravy over my jeans.

I bent down to lick them clean,
Until my mother started to scream.

Next to go was apple pie,
I threw it up towards the sky.

It hit the ceiling with such a thud
And came down like sticky mud.

Over my dad and over my mum,
This meal was turning out to be fun.

Here comes my dog, Mable,
Oops! She just ate the table.

This is the end of my poem of nonsense,
But it will always be on my conscience.

Eleanor Stimpson (10)
St Peter's RC Primary School, Winchester

WEATHER

January start again,
Winter whiteness,
Snow and rain.

February fires glowing,
Frost and fogs,
Bitter winds blowing.

March starts the leaves off growing
The start of spring,
Boats are rowing.

April showers pouring in,
Roots dig down
And plants begin.

May brings happiness to all,
Foals stand up,
Grass breaks their fall.

June brings sun's hottest time,
Waving grass,
Scent of pine.

July brings joyful times,
Seeing aunties,
Telling rhymes.

August brings the beating sun,
Seaside castle,
Lots of fun.

September means back to school,
Working hard,
Weekends rule!

October brings dark black nights,
Hallowe'en is close,
What eerie sights!

November fireworks in the sky,
Pretty colours,
Flying high.

December Christmas shopping time,
Turkey cooking,
Church bells chime.

January start again . . .

Alice Egerton-Kemp (9)
St Peter's RC Primary School, Winchester

THE STORM

The great storm;
It rules the sky -
Scary, massive, mighty,
Like a body covering the sky;
Like a huge rollercoaster.
It makes me feel small -
Like a flea in elephant land.
The great storm;
Reminds us how weak we are.

Thomas Anderson (10)
St Peter's RC Primary School, Winchester

A POEM

The piper led the rats to the river
The eerie tune made them quiver
He heard a splash
And then a crash
As they all lost their lives with a shiver.

Leon Sherwood (10)
St Peter's RC Primary School, Winchester

GUESS WHAT!

My
  Cat
   Is
    A

Nine lifer,
  Roof rider,
Food taker,
  Fluff maker,
Moonlight kisser,
  And guess what! My cat is a
Big hisser!

Sarah McLaren (9)
St Peter's RC Primary School, Winchester

SQUIRREL

Nut collector,
Tree spoiler,
Bushy tailed,
Food fetcher,
Deep digger,
Garden wrecker,
Wide-eyed,
Seriously clever.

Charlotte Rose (10)
St Peter's RC Primary School, Winchester

JANUARY ARRIVES

January is here
Outside in the blistering wind
Rosy cheeks and chattering teeth.
It's grey and misty, hard to see
The slippery surfaces icy as can be.
Oh the fun of wrapping up warm
Out in the garden the spiky, frozen lawn.
A child cries 'Help!'
After falling off the sledge, then yelp.
The thick snow laying
Upon the arms of the tree saying
'Oh what beastly weather today
No one is outside to play.'

Verity McGrath (11)
St Swithun's RC Primary School, Southsea

GIRLS AND GUYS

A guy met a girl
His eyes went whirl,
The guy brought her presents
And took her to his parents,
And the girl bought him presents
And took him to her parents.
Then one night they sat on a log
And guess what happened?
They had a snog!

Hadleigh Sanchez-Harrison (11)
St Swithun's RC Primary School, Southsea

THE WORLD BELOW

The sun burns with anger in its eyes,
It shines upon the hundreds of lost creatures,
Running around in the busy cities.
It hides behind the lost secrets
Of the clouds as if it's scared
Of the drumming from the world below.

Prunella Jones (11)
St Swithun's RC Primary School, Southsea

WHAT IS BLACK?

Black is the colour of the suits they wear at funerals.
Black is the depth of space just like a person from another human race.
Black is like black hair just like a nightmare.
Black is a shadow just like a burned meadow.
Black is like coal just like a small mole.
Where would we be without black?

James Price (10)
St Swithun's RC Primary School, Southsea

THE POEM OF AUTUMN

The autumn wind blows gently upon the fallen leaves.
The animals gathering food for their hibernation.
The conker trees are dropping their bombs from the sky.
The apples are disappearing one by one like each drop of falling rain.
When it comes to the end of the day the wolf howling out like the noise
Of a woman calling for help.

Jack Hardcastle (10)
St Swithun's RC Primary School, Southsea

GLOOM

Blow out the fire in my heart
Let the tears run from my face
Rub out the days of the week,
And let the mourners mourn.

Let the sun burn out
And let the moon melt
Stop all of the stars from shining
And let the mourners mourn.

Let the spirits wonder
And let the angels weep.
You were the only one I loved
And the only one I should keep.
They say every cloud has a silver lining,
But what good can come of this?

Siobhan Swords (10)
St Swithun's RC Primary School, Southsea

THE CLEAR SEA

I was under the sea
Jumping dolphins, jumping whales,
Mermaids swimming, mermaids sitting,
A sunken boat, fish use as a play area.
At the bottom of the calm ocean sea
All you could see was sand, the sea was rocky, the sea was wavy
Tunnels, dolphins and whales play in
Dolphins and whales squeaking like guinea pigs.

Faye Graeney (10)
St Swithun's RC Primary School, Southsea

WINTER

Winter is here
It puts everything into a mysterious trance.
Winter dances among the skinny trees, covering them in her jewels.
The freezing winds whip harshly through the night
And course through the alleyways like a dragon.
As a lost soul tries to find its way through the deserted streets,
Ponds cry out for help from beneath their icy prisons.
Even though winter grasps all in his hand,
Spring with all her might shall conquer him.
When a frost-bitten person stumbles home
The trees reach out for they have no place to go.
But no matter how loudly winter roars like a wounded animal
The fire crackles merrily as the cat stretches out in front of it,
To sleep, sleep.

Joseph Weston (10)
St Swithun's RC Primary School, Southsea

A TROPICAL DAY

The sun rises, morning comes,
Making the day not dark but bright
Cool, tropical water laps against the golden beach.
Crabs scurry sideways, hiding in the seaweed and rocks.
Palm trees curve round creating a small patch of shade.
The sun falls, leaving a black velvet blanket,
Small stars flicker like a flame that could live forever.

Greta Start (10)
St Swithun's RC Primary School, Southsea

CAT

A cat is an elegant, slinky creature
With bright, green eyes
Reflecting the pale moonlight.
She is strange and mysterious,
A secretive animal
With a locked-up soul.
Eyes like flickering, sparkling emeralds,
Shiny, silky black coat,
Long, winding, curling tail
Her razor-sharp claws are pointed,
They're shining silver swords
Glinting catching your eye.

Daisy Reeves (10)
St Swithun's RC Primary School, Southsea

WHAT IS GREEN?

Green is the colour of nature.
Green is the colour of grass.
Green is the colour of fresh leaves.
Green is the colour of tops of trees.
Green is the colour of peas.
Green is the guardian of nature and peace.
Green is the colour of a fresh apple.
Green is the colour of most walls and houses.
Green is all over the world.
But what would happen without it?

Denis De Lucas (10)
St Swithun's RC Primary School, Southsea

JANUARY DAWNS

January dawns, howling wind, noses are red, teeth a-chattering
The trees branches are like arms preparing to fight.
The snow is falling, frozen ponds.
Wrapping up warm playing on the front lawn.
The leaves are skipping along the path to a cosy cottage.
The grey and misty streets are empty
No one dare fight the monstrous storm.
The rain is like a sobbing child never wanting to stop
The bushes are angry dragons just awoken by the bitter air
The headlights of a car are human eyes glaring at you through
                                          the foggy sky
Be full of fear for the winter monster is here.

Rhianne Thomas (11)
St Swithun's RC Primary School, Southsea

JANUARY

As you step outside the biting cold hits you like a bear raging and angry
The howling winds freeze you to the spot
The smoke steams out of the chimney, desperately fighting the warmth
                                          against the bitter cold.
The deserted land left alone
Snow untouched like a white, velvet sea
The land is asleep not alive anymore
But there's nothing to fear
For spring is near.

Alyssia Broomfield (11)
St Swithun's RC Primary School, Southsea

Hard January

January is here again, these nights of huddling around a glowing fire
Toasting marshmallows and drinking huge mugs of hot chocolate
Defrosting fingers and toes after a brisk walk out.

Bed time again, gingerly climbing into bed
Clutching my hot water bottle
As if a thief would enter and take it.

As I wake from my now cosy nest
I open my eyes to my dark, unfriendly room
Just five minutes longer, but it seems like one minute.

Bravely I dress,
I can hear the cries of the wind outside battering the trees
Not long before I will be out there.

Dressed in my snug hat, scarf and gloves I step out
To feel the biting cold nip my cheeks and nose
I skate down the road on the slippery ice and pass other people
                                        with the same rosy cheeks
As if like walking snowmen.

Snow starts to fall and I see my friends coming towards me
We laugh together as we try to catch the snowflakes.

Maybe January isn't so bad after all.

Rachael Bull (11)
St Swithun's RC Primary School, Southsea

THE ZOO

Going to the zoo is a very special treat
Unusual animals I know we'll soon meet
Monkeys, gorillas and chimpanzees,
It's fun to see them swinging through trees.
Zebras are stripy all black and white
Giraffes can reach tops of trees, alright!
Lions and tigers are extremely scary,
Big brown bears, very hairy!
Huge elephants with long trunks,
Peacocks with feathers, hair like punks.
Hyenas laughing happy with glee,
Penguins underwater, fast as can be.
Going to the zoo is so much fun,
The day went so quickly it is now done.

Emily Clayson (10)
South Wonston Primary School

WHY ME?

Why do you stand and stare?
Why do you look round?
I am just sitting here on the corner of the street
Begging for money.
My child may be sick
But don't just look,
Can't you just walk by and not stand and stare?
I am a beggar, you can see that well
But don't think I am different
I am just like you
But don't stand and stare.

James Kukla (9)
South Wonston Primary School

THE THUNDER

I can rumble through the night without being seen,
    And I can frighten all kinds of children; medium, fat or lean.

I can fight and beat the lightning, without even a scar,
    And I can really frighten a driver, so he ends up crashing his car.

I can drive the clouds in front of the sun,
    And warn the people that the lightning will come.

But when I'm angry you'd better watch out,
    For my growling voice to bawl out a shout.

Soon there'll be floods all over the world,
    And I'll be here snuggled and curled.

The rain may pour, though I shall stay dry,
    And down below, people ask why.

I can wake up Neptune, god of the sea,
    And make him make waves, while I laugh with glee.

Tomorrow is misery for the people below,
    But life up here gleams and glows!

Cassandre Robson (10)
South Wonston Primary School

TOM TICKLE

Tom Tickle saved a pickle from a nasty nickel
He tickled the nasty nickel
Who then let go of the pickle
And was kicked by Tom Tickle,
Who was thanked by the pickle,
Who was saved from that nasty nickel.

Jacinta Gardner (11)
South Wonston Primary School

WHY ME?

Alone on the streets one sunny day,
Nothing to be happy for on this day in May,
In my world it's raining and grey,
It's turning dark and what do you see?
You see me, me that's what you see.

You go home and snuggle in your bed,
While I sit here with my dog Ned,
What do you see? What do you see?
You see me, me, that's what you see.

Nothing to eat, nothing to drink,
I feel like I want to be swallowed down a sink,
I sit here with a hat or a cap
Thinking me, me, why me?
Me alone in this vast unfriendly world,
That's what you see, me, me, that's what you see.

Lauren Russell (9)
South Wonston Primary School

THE WIND

I can get angry as a lion
Just like that,
Happy as a butterfly,
Gentle as a cat.
I can rattle all the windows,
Smash all the glass,
And then be a cold breeze,
In summer, at last.

James Cuell (10)
South Wonston Primary School

SPIDER IN THE SHADOWS

Scuttling towards me like a ghost
I jumped up on the sofa
Looking up with its beady eyes
Scaly, dragon-skin body
I let out a cry
It padded under the sofa
Like a spy.
I was petrified out of my wits
I could not move a muscle
I tried my best to scream
But hang on I think it was a dream
I flopped out of bed yawning
And then I saw it.
I dived on to the sofa screaming for help
It scurried underneath
Waiting . . .

Waiting to pounce.

Matthew Harvey (9)
South Wonston Primary School

WHY ME?

Why, why, why is it always me?
Whenever I walk out of my house
With a bag there is always someone
Who thinks, there is that black girl again
Trying to nick something.
My mum is white and my dad is black
That means I'm no different to you.
Wouldn't the world be a better place if nobody was racist?

Louise Peacock (8)
South Wonston Primary School

THE FROST

He left his white hand prints on the window panes peering into the
                                                    bright room,
His delicate footprints laid a white blanket of talcum powder
                                                    on the ground,
The trees were covered in silver glitter that sparkled in the moonlight.
A white sheet of petals covered rooftops where birds made cold nests.
A thick glass of ice covered roads, lakes, seas and ponds,
An old man's beard covered birds food and blocked squirrels in
A cold, soft and thick layer of cotton wool covered the rooftops
                                                    of old people's garages,
The gutters were filled with white, glossy toothpaste
With candyfloss softly settled on children's wendy houses.
This poem is about the reign of the frost.

Charlotte West (11)
South Wonston Primary School

MY DOG POLLY

I can bark and bark all night long,
Or I can scratch the door and cry a song.
I can see next door's cat climbing a pole,
While I finish off the leftovers that were in my bowl.
I can feel the warmth of the cosy house,
Looking out of the window at the cat and a mouse.
I can see the flames of the homely fire,
When I lay in my basket the shape of a tyre.

Beth Parsons (10)
South Wonston Primary School

IT'S ONLY WORDS

It's hard to say the things I feel
My thoughts move fast
My words are slow
Feelings held by the words I know.

Hurt or happy, proud or disappointed
Pain and sorrow make me cry
Smiles and jokes make laugh
My feelings though cut words in half.

Cave man art tells of the world
No words are used to tell the story.
A good book paints a clear scene
Our language fills the gaps between.

Jack Dubben (11)
South Wonston Primary School

WHITE, FLUFFY CANDYFLOSS

White, fluffy candyfloss
Floating in the sky.

White, fluffy candyfloss
Slowly passing by.

White, fluffy candyfloss
Spreading up and high.

White, fluffy candyfloss
Learning how to fly.

Hollie Amato (10)
South Wonston Primary School

THE RUNAWAY MERRY-GO-ROUND HORSE

Standing in the circle, different from all the rest
A robin sat on the fence and ruffled his red, red chest
All the other horses were white or mellow brown
This different one I sat on and galloped into town
It really did surprise me and yet so suddenly
He galloped down a steep, steep hill and off tumbled me!

Chantal Partridge (11)
South Wonston Primary School

STARS

Stars are twinkling stars
They come very close to Mars,
You can catch them in jars,
And put them in cars,
Lovely, twinkling stars.

Lauren Weatherall (10)
South Wonston Primary School

SUNFLOWER

I elegantly stand
My head towering over you
With breathtaking coloured petals
I stun you with my radiance,
My petals are like the colour of sand
In the wind I make no sound
My roots as an anchor in the ground.

Rochell Lant (10)
South Wonston Primary School

NIGHT FRIGHT

As I wander the dark streets at night,
The glow of the moon is my only light.
When I hear a noise from behind my ear,
The whole of my body quivers with fear.
As a werewolf howls and a phantom floats,
An icy hand seems to clutch at my throat.
Then an owl hoots loudly and gives out a whine
And a shiver of fear creeps up my spine.
I look all around but I've lost my way,
I wish and wish for the break of day.
I start to run and close my eyes,
Hoping to find somewhere I recognise.
But I'm now in a forest so dark and bleak,
With none of the help that I try to seek.
As I wait here thinking evil creatures circle around,
I stand as a statue, hardly breathing,
Not making a sound.
The vampire's fangs are as sharp as knives,
I beg for the monsters to spare my life.
Dragons, goblins, witches and their cats,
Giants, banshees, spectres and bats.
To my amazement a light appears in the sky,
A white light so bright I shield my eyes.
A dazzling unicorn soars like a dove,
A heavenly sight when you're looking above.
It rescues me quickly and we fly towards the moon,
I hope to be back at home very soon.
I see the monsters behind and I let out a scream,
But I wake up to find it was only a dream.

Lizzie McLoughlin (10)
South Wonston Primary School

MY DREAM WORLD

In my world the sofas are islands covered in golden sand
My fish pond's the sea which I splash with my hand
My building blocks are a magic castle with winding staircase.
My daddy is a giant with huge shoes and ropy laces
My downstairs cupboard is a bear cave deep and dark
And my budgie is a swift, golden lark.
My doggy is a dragon with deep, fiery breath
And my garden is a maze with rights and lefts.
My mummy is a fairy dancing through the leaves
And my kitchen is the forest with deep tall trees
But my favourite place to be when it gets cold and dark
Is curling up in a flower or my duvet in my cosy, cuddly bed in the
dark.

Charlotte Mercer (11)
South Wonston Primary School

SAD!

I'm sad and unhappy
With no one to care
I lie in the dark and look and stare
I've been banished forever under the bed
I wait with the sock and the old piece of bread,
Until the day comes when the sad, lonely feeling
Will be gone as I'm loosing that feeling.
When I'm taken out and someone new looks and stares,
As I'll be a new little teddy bear.

Jennifer Hornby (10)
South Wonston Primary School

NIGHT

It's night-time,
It's night-time,
Go to bed,
Don't bump your head.
Hear the hedgehogs in the leaves,
Hear the wind,
Hear the breeze.
Go to sleep
Don't sneeze.
It's night-time,
It's night-time.
Night is gone,
Now it's morning.

Kate Henley (8)
Stockbridge Primary School

IT'S A CAT'S LIFE

Sleeping, snuggling, curling up tight,
Eating, cleaning, hunting all night,
Running, swirling, jumping into flight,
Watching, waiting, chasing mice in fright.

A cat's life, that's right.

Jordana Jayne (10)
Stockbridge Primary School

UNTITLED

I made a paper plane really quick,
It would not fly, not one bit.
Perhaps it wasn't quite so slick,
Because it made it much too quick.
Next time I'll take my time a bit.

Sam Hofman (9)
Stockbridge Primary School

ALIENS

One night I was looking through my telescope,
When I saw something whizz across the sky
It stopped quickly above my front drive,
I saw it land, suddenly a platform whooshed out.

Loads of armed aliens came out on the long platform
They were about six feet tall, their bodies were green,
On their triangular shaped heads were two huge black eyes,
There was a boss in the middle draped with red silk.

They walked slowly up the path to our wooden front door
Two of the armed aliens came and rocked the front door down
All of the aliens came up the stairs and came in my bedroom
The boss said 'We have come from Mars.

We are going to invade and destroy all life on earth,
You are going to be the very first to die.' 'No-o!'
I said, I quickly turned on some pop music,
The aliens went mad their heads exploded,
I've saved the world, I thought happily.

Callum O'Neill (9)
Velmead Junior School

SOUNDS AT THE PARK

The bark of the dog.
The click of the old ladies knitting needles.
The rustle of the squirrel leaping in the leaves.
The tweet of the bird chirping to the other birds.
The whistle of the man calling his friendly dog.
These are some sounds of the park
The flap of the white dove's wings.

The crackle of the leaves falling.
The bounce of the red shiny ball.
The chatter of the people next door.
The thud of the children's feet racing to the swings.
The cry of the hungry baby lying on the bench.
They're the sounds of the park.

The click,
The bark,
The rustle,
The tweet,
The whistle,
The flap,
The bounce,
The chat,
The thud,
The cry,
I can hear them all when I'm going home.

Helen Sutherland (7)
Velmead Junior School

SOUND POEM

I wake in my bed,
Wakey, wakey says my mum waking me up.
I hear people singing on the radio.
I hear the shower dripping drip, drop
Then I hear the kettle boiling a few minutes later.
I hear my toast popping out of the toaster.
I hear my sister eating her breakfast, crunch.
I hear my mum blowing on her tea, blow.
Then I hear my sister brushing her teeth,
Then I hear my mum starting the car, brum,
When I go outside I hear the cat purring, purr,
Then I hear children laughing.
Then I hear the bus stop, chhhh,
I hear the children shouting on the bus,
And then I hear the children draw on the window.

Anna Phillips (8)
Velmead Junior School

SNOWFLAKES

S   oft, sparkling snow falling down,
N   othing but snow spreads across the ground.
O   ver the rooftops, sheets of dazzling white
W   ow! Never seen it so bright!
F   lakes of snow look like stars,
L   ittle bright drops all the way to Mars.
A   ll the children go out to play
K   nowing they'll have a fantastic day!
E   ach tiny, dazzling, white snowflake
S   parkles to keep all snowmen awake!

Nicole Chapman (8)
Velmead Junior School

SOUNDS

In the classroom,
Pens screeching, girls singing, boys humming,
Pencil sharpeners crunching.
Outside in the playground,
Balls smashing and crashing into the window
Chains off swings tingle, trees crunching in the wind
And cars and buses rumbling.
On the beach,
Waves crashing on to the shore, people talking,
Crabs clicking with their pincers, fish splashing,
Kids splashing, clams clapping under the water
                              and whales hum and echo.

James Pardy (8)
Velmead Junior School

DREAM ISLAND

D ream Island is a spectacular place
R olling noises are hard to hear
E verywhere noises tremble up my lace
A nd the trees are very strange,
M any people like them.

I don't, I don't, but they're top range
S ometimes they're brilliant,
L ook around what do you see?
A nimals, animals in the island,
N ever mind I'm still me
D ream, dream what do you see?

Alice Gribble (8)
Velmead Junior School

MY TEACHER

My teacher is an alien,
She only eats Mars bars
She makes it look so easy
Eating twenty motor cars.

I'll prove she is an alien
She's twenty-one feet tall
The next day she came in
She banged her big head on the wall.

She hasn't got an address,
Nor a postcode,
She hasn't got a pet,
Except an old smelly toad.

I hope you listened well,
This poem is quite true,
And if you ever see her house,
Tell me, please do.

Martha Paton (9)
Velmead Junior School

DOGS

Barking dogs,
Hunting for the rabbits,
Lasting energy still to burn out.

The wet nose tracking down the baby deer.
I see it,
I see it.

Daniel Sculler (8)
Velmead Junior School

STARS

Huge,
Flashing,
Colourful,
Silver,
Glittering,
Shining,
Sparkling,
Flying far,
Shooting.

Still,
Comes out at night,
Sparkles in the night,
Flying across the sky.

Peter Mancktelow (8)
Velmead Junior School

SOUTH AFRICAN ANIMALS

Cheetahs with yellow skin, black spots and speed,
Now the cheetah creeps up on the impala.
Drinking the aquamarine blue water
As the sun beats on his back
Closer, closer!
The race is on!
Now the impala, dodges and turns in fear
Will the cheetah win?

Daniel Rodgett (8)
Velmead Junior School

FARM SOUNDS

The pink pig bellowed very loud, oink, oink
As he roles in the mud
Moo shrieks the black and white cow
As she is just being led to the milking stable.

Baa, baa, baa screams the sheep,
Having his woolly coat cut.
Quack, quack, says the duck
Splashing in the pond.

Neigh, neigh sang the horse,
Being ridden round the field.
Cock-a-doodle-do went the cockerel
Waking everybody up.

Laura Cobb (9)
Velmead Junior School

NIGHT-TIME

Nothing is more beautiful than the night sky
I hear the twinkle of the stars shining up in the air so high.
Great big blows of wind come through the door.
Then I hear the moon start to twinkle even more.
You hear the wind start to whine
I climb into bed and there is not a line
My door is shut so I rest my head
Every day waiting for another night in my bed.

Anna Musgrove (9)
Velmead Junior School

RAIN, THUNDER AND LIGHTNING

Crash, goes the thunder
Bang goes the lightning.
The rain falls on my head,
It is freezing cold
I walk through the wet creepy night,
All I can hear is pitter, patter, pitter, patter,
On my head.
I go upstairs,
It is dark and dingy upstairs
I try not to be scared but I can't help it
I try to go to sleep . . .
I finally did.

Sophie Malone (9)
Velmead Junior School

THE SEA

Dark foggy, blue across the waves
Strong hard waves blowing away
Rocky rocks sharp as T-Rex teeth.
Amazing sand under water
The smell of seaweed on the water
Ships fade away in the fog
Whoop goes the horn of the boats
Roar, goes the sound of the sea.

Simon Jenkins (9)
Velmead Junior School

WEATHER IN A WEEK

Monday, it's snowing,
Brr, brr, brr.

Tuesday, it's raining,
Quick under cover everybody!

Wednesday, it's thunder and lightning,
Ahh, ahh.

Thursday, it's sunny,
Mum, it's really hot!

Friday, it's icy
Ahh, *slippery!*

Weather in a week.

Gemma Bussey (9)
Velmead Junior School

DAYS OF THE WEEK

Monday, warm, hot, sunny day.
Tuesday, dazzling, dramatic, summery day.
Wednesday, cars crashing, trucks smashing on the icy roads.
Thursday blistering cold, no time to play.
Oh that's
Friday out on the sleigh time to play is blistering cold.
Is nine o'clock time to go to bed.

Sam Heal (9)
Velmead Junior School

THE STRANGE SOUND

There's a strange sound in our house,
It's not like the ticking of an antiquated clock
Or the whizzing washing machine rotating the clothes,
It doesn't sound like the steady beat of the dripping of a tap.

There's a strange sound in our house,
It's not the yelling of a mad baby
Or the squeaking of an angry parrot,
It doesn't sound like the loud ringing of the doorbell.

There's a strange sound in our house,
It's not the barking of a hungry dog
Or the clattering of the milkman placing bottles by the door
It doesn't sound like the meowing of my cat.

There's a strange sound in our house,
It's not the scuttling of my lonely hamster
Or the shutting of a door,
It's not the flush of the upstairs toilet
Or the yelling of my crazy mum,
There's a strange sound in our house . . .

Zoë Cox-Putker (8)
Velmead Junior School

RACE ME

R ace me, I bet I'll win
A nd by the way your head will be in that bin.
C an I win? Can I loose?
E asy peasy cheers for me and boos for you.

M aybe I'll lose, maybe I won't
E choes shout *no you don't.*

Jasmine Knight (8)
Velmead Junior School

HAMSTER

Hamster, hamster in its bed
Hamster has a tiny head,
Hamster, hamster is so cool, playing
                        with its tiny ball.

Hamster, hamster kissing head,
Hamster, hamster time for bed.
Hamster, hamster wake up time,
Now it has just gone past nine.

Hamster, hamster, hamster!

Hamster, hamster rest your head,
Hamster, hamster out of bed.
Hamster play the day away,
Hamster play, play all day.

Hamster had a busy day,
Hamster lay down on the hay.

Charlie Titchmarsh (9)
Velmead Junior School

ALIENS

The aliens are green,
Ugly,
Cool,
Fat,
Spies,
Lovely,
The aliens are spotless.

Kieren Martin (9)
Velmead Junior School

THE SPACE ROCKET

When I watch TV
And see a space rocket launching
It reaches high in the air
Before disappearing.

I've never been in a rocket
But I think it must be scary
If something goes wrong
Or crashing into the ocean.

Soon after the rocket
The shuttle was invented
There wasn't any thrill
And the space rocket wasn't used again.

Oliver Richards (8)
Velmead Junior School

MONSTERS

M   onsters, monsters everywhere,
O   gres hitting people with big clubs,
N   aughty gnomes wrecking people's gardens
S   piders making silken webs all over the place,
T   rolls running around with hammers,
E   lves roaming the forests with imps,
R   ats smelling of sewage,
S   cary monsters going to bed till tomorrow night.

Matthew Wareham (9)
Velmead Junior School

My Imagination

Imagine if you could sail a storm or have a new baby born.
Imagine going to see Steps or look after hundreds of pets.
Imagine a secret garden whilst stones harden.
Imagine being a bird where no one is heard.
Imagine being a pop star when you go too far.
Imagine, imagine.

Imagine stepping into a book with a big, fat crook.
Imagine a trip to Egypt and buy a souvenir and keep it.
Imagine discovering an ancient object or give it a groovy effect.

John Southgate (9)
Velmead Junior School

Weather

Tornadoes twisting, twirling,
Hurricanes hyper, hurling,
Stormy, stirred storms,
Typhoons terrorising while another forms.

Rain drip, drop, dripping
Leaves flip, flop, flipping,
Sunlight dancing,
Snowflakes prancing.

Thunder hitting,
Lightning ear splitting,
Snow falling,
And underneath people are bawling.

Patrick Couldwell (8)
Velmead Junior School

ICE CREAM

Ice cream is cold
It melts in your mouth
You get all different flavours
Can you feel it running down your throat?

Vanilla, chocolate, strawberry,
Raspberry, mint, honeycomb,
Blueberry, lemon, nut,
Orange, milk, toffee.

Ice cream is freezing
When you eat ice cream
Your mouth goes all numb
I love ice cream.

Ice cream, ice cream,
Everywhere I love ice cream
It's the best
Ice cream!

Shelby Carter (9)
Velmead Junior School

DOG STUFF

Dogs bark very loudly
Outside they will run and run
Getting faster, beating everyone
Soft dogs by the fire
Then he will sleep for the night
Up the next morning
'Fun being with you' said the dog.

Millie Campbell (8)
Velmead Junior School

HAUNT HOUSE

I ran down the spooky path,
Which led me to a haunted house,
With a huge, black, creepy door,
With spiders painted on the wall.

I bang on the door,
But no one was home,
So I pushed the door open
And it crashes on the wall.

I stepped inside the haunted house,
It was quite dark and dingy,
There is no light at all,
Bang!

The door was shut,
It made me jump,
Help, help, I shout,
But no one comes.

I run to the door,
But it was stuck,
So I gave it a kick,
And the door was opened.

I ran down the spooky path,
Which led me home.

Jasmine Spragg (9)
Velmead Junior School

SOUNDS OF WINTER

The rain going plick plock on my scalp,
The bumping of the foggy clouds,
The red hot sneezy nose going bless you,
The call of the blowing wind in the freezing village,
The emerald green trees going swish, swosh in the breeze,
The curtains going whisk, whoosh,
The sore throat cough, cough,
The gleaming, yellow lighting cool, *flash, bang, pop,*
The splashy full puddles,
The slippery cold snow,
The sun comes out after the storm is over,
The summer has come.
When is winter coming again?

Amy Blanchard (8)
Velmead Junior School

SOUNDS IN THE ZOO

Baa says the black sheep,
Neigh says the brown horse kicking his back leg.
Roar roars the lion in a loud voice.
The long neck giraffe eats from the tallest tree in the zoo.
The elephant splashes water at us that makes a splishing sound.
The snap of the crocodile makes me scared.
The knocking of the woodpecker makes a dent in the tree.
The cuckoo of the cuckoo makes me feel like I am in a clock.
The bright colour of the parrot makes me feel bright.

Ruth Simmons (8)
Velmead Junior School

WWF Wrestling

Wrestling can be entertaining
It could end your career.
You're standing in the wrestling arena
The crowd are screaming
You're down on the floor
The referee is counting 1, 2, but you kick out.

You get back up
You're really scared and you want to lose
But you really want the World Wrestling Federation title
You're bleeding.

You pin your enemy,
The referee counts 1, 2, 3, and you win the match
The crowd are screaming like they've never screamed before.

James Wilde (9)
Velmead Junior School

The Sound Bag

As I look in the lonely bag
I see the squeak of a mouse,
The first word of a baby,
The magic song of a bird,
A lion about to kill its prey,
The first sparkle of raindrops,
Flowers going down for winter,
The whistling of the wind,
The scream of trees as children hit them.

Megan O'Connor (7)
Velmead Junior School

SOUNDS AT HOME

The clicking of the ladder,
The creaking of the stairs,
The ticking of the clock,
The dinging of the bell,
The talking of the radio,
The growling of the bear,
The barking of the dog,
All the noises are so loud,
The squealing of the baby waiting for its dinner,
The rustling of people stepping on leaves,
The sizzling of the frying pan,
The dinging of the door bell,
These are the noises you hear at home.

Andrew Woodruff (7)
Velmead Junior School

SOUNDS IN SCHOOL

Chatter go the children,
Bang goes the heavy door,
Creak goes the Velcro,
Swish goes the brown paintbrush,
Click goes the gel pen top,
Slam goes the front cover of the dictionary,
HB pencils being dropped on the table,
With all of these sounds I think my ears are about to burst!
Bang!

Ryan Nisbet (8)
Velmead Junior School

RACE

One night I went in the closet
A light flashed, I was scared
I found myself in a race
And I tripped over a giant lead.

I don't know why I was here
I tell you it was like a dream
I ran down a hill
Cheered by a football team.

Something was making me run
I fell down a hill
Rolling, rolling, rolling
I saw the Rugrat Lil!

I climbed up a rainbow
I saw a river like wind
A world of magical leaves
I felt like I was pinned.

I could see the finish line from here
I could not get down
I fell through the finish line
I was astonished I could have drowned.

I woke in my bed
The closet was at its normal ways
Was it true?
I found a small graze.

Kurt Jones (9)
Velmead Junior School

THE SEASIDE

When I go to the seaside
The crabs grab my toes
The dolphins jump in the sea
And the waves crash on the sand.

The jellyfish sting people
The seals bob up and down
The surfers stand on their surf boards
And babies get lost in the sea.

The seagulls wake you in the morning
The body boarders fly down the beach
The rock pools are full of shrimps
And the sun makes everything hot.

The shells get collected by children
The fish get collected in buckets
Sand castles are made in the sand
And my mum has a nap on a towel.

When I go to the seaside
The crabs grab my toes
The dolphins jump in the sea
And the waves crash on the sand.

Sarah Woolley (8)
Velmead Junior School

SAMMY SNAKE

Sammy the slimy snake
Slid down the stairs
Into my mum's pyjamas.

Emily Wood (9)
Wallop Primary School

CARS

Look at all the cars that people drive
Red ones, green ones, dirty ones and clean ones.

Up and down the roads and on the motorway,
In and out the towns and in the countryside.

Look at all the scrappy cars rusting in a heap.

Look at all the smart cars parked in driveways and in the towns.

Look at all the people starring when they're around,
I wish I had one and I bet you
Do too!

David Floyd (11)
Wallop Primary School

THE SPACE ROCKET

The midnight rocket
Standing in floodlights
Crew looking down
Waiting for the flight.

The rocket takes off
Into the ink, black sky
To the giant moon
We continuously fly.

There goes Mercury,
There goes Mars,
Weightlessly drifting
On through the stars.

Luke Wells (10)
Wallop Primary School

TORNADOES

Tornadoes, tornadoes are fast and furious
Zooming around not a care in the
World, destroying and killing,
Crushing and burying,
Anything in its way.
The sizes can vary,
From tiny to giant,
And can affect
The world to
Fix the mess,
Mother
Nature
Has
Left
Behind.

Thomas Abraham (10)
Wallop Primary School

THE SUN

The sun is glowing in the sky
Like a shining, sparkling butterfly
The sun is sparkling on the waves.

The boats sway and sway
Like bats in a cave.

The sun is beating down on the ground
When we are playing football all round
Then the sun fades away
And comes another day.

Sam Waite (11)
Wallop Primary School

POOR HAMPION

There was a bee called Hampion
Who was always the champion.
One day in a race,
He forgot about the chase
And that was the end of the champion!

Tom Baker (9)
Wallop Primary School

LOVE BIRDS

There is a bird called Robin
With a big, fat friend called Dobbin.
Robin fell in love
With a fat collar dove
And Dobbin was jealous of Robin.

Samantha Andrews (8)
Wallop Primary School

ROB'S DOG

There was a man called Rob
Who had a big gob.
One day he got a dog
Who was called Hog
Silly old Rob.

Thomas Skerratt (9)
Wallop Primary School

SUNNY AND THE BUNNY

There was a dog called Sunny
Who loved to eat honey.
One day she was chasing a bunny
To try to get back her money
She looked so funny chasing a bunny.

Gemma Brotherwood (9)
Wallop Primary School

MY SISTER

I have a sister
Who has a blister
It's on her back
So she wears a sack.
What a silly sister.

Chelsea Smith (8)
Wallop Primary School

MAN FROM SCADOOTER

There was once a man form Scadooter
Who tried to ride his scooter
But to his disgust
The stupid thing's bust
And he caught his foot in the hooter!

Joe Wells (8)
Wallop Primary School

THE BERMUDA TRIANGLE

The Bermuda Triangle is a deadly place,
Only people who dare to cross, cross,
But when they cross, they find that they'll never see each other again.

Many things have happened in the Bermuda Triangle
From Christopher Columbus and his amazing ship
To flight 19 and its twenty-seven men.
There are about two hundred others.

The weather was bad for flight 19
The captain's compass went haywire
Then they went trundling to Jar
Which sent them to the bottom of the ocean.

People say it's under surveillance by aliens
Which would explain the missing flight 19
And Christopher Columbus' missing Marie Celeste.
This will always be a mystery for the scientists
And nobody knows what will happen next.

Scot Robertson (10)
Wallop Primary School

WILD DREAMS

Last night I imagined that the boys were octopuses,
And the girls were cacti.
The teachers were giant dinosaurs,
The assembly hall was a tortoise shell,
The classrooms were giant coconut shells,
The playgrounds were skin,
The fields were spiders' webs.
Then I woke up, thank goodness.

Ryan Smith (7)
Wallop Primary School

WIND AND RAIN

There was a young girl from Monder
Who liked to walk when it was windier
She was clowning around
When her trousers fell down
And nobody wanted to see her.

The girl had a dad called Blain
Who went for a walk in the rain
Then the wind blew
And off his coat flew
And he never liked rain again.

Jack Barnes (8)
Wallop Primary School

A GHOST CALLED PAUL

There was a young ghost called Paul
Who was no good at skullball at all.
He hit his own striker,
Three zombies and a biker
The only thing safe was the skull.

After he'd played skullball
All of his team said 'You stupid fool.'
So then he went back to bed
Where he lived in coffins with the dead
Then he woke up much later in a church hall.

Nicholas Forbes (9)
Wallop Primary School

WE HAVE A DREAM

We have a dream of no pollution,
Of clean fields with tons of grass.
We have a dream of floating cars,
In the millenniums that are to pass.

We have a dream of spaceships landing,
Of aliens talking with the human race.
We have a dream of different planets,
Of comets flying straight from space.

Many of us have a dream often,
With our ideas tossing to and fro.
But what will happen we'll just have to wait,
For the future we will never know.

Sarah V Musgrove (9)
Wallop Primary School

PEACE

The world at the moment is a very scary place
People make fun of other people's race,
But most people want all fighting to cease,
Most people just want peace.

Some people cause war,
I don't want any more,
This world should be free,
For you and for me.

I just want peace.

Mark Heffernan (10)
Wallop Primary School

ALPHABETICAL POEM

Andy the angry antelope ate an apple.
Billy the bad bear brought a ball.
Carter the crazy cat likes climbing curtains.
Dilly the dirty donkey dives into the dinner.
Emily the elephant likes eating.
Freddy the funny frog fell through the floor.
Gary the goose likes gambling.
Hannah the hairy horse hates homework.
Incy the Indian crashed into the igloo.
James the jolly jaguar jumped over the jumper.
Kerry the killing kite killed the king.
Lucy the loud lemur likes leaping on leopards.
Megan the mean mouse met a mummy.
Naughty Nigel doesn't clean his nails.
Ollie the orange only likes the colour orange.
Polly the poorly parrot bumped into the past.
Queen Quite is very quiet.
Roger the rabbit is a robber.
Silly Sally saw a sea-saw.
Terry was terrified when tiny Tom came.
Unlucky umbrellas had to go to university.
Vicky the vampire sucks up vacuum cleaners.
     Wilfred the warthog went to wash his warts.
Xylophones like having X-rays at X-mas.
Yellow yachts like doing yoga.
Zoe the zebra likes the zoo.

Stacey Ruddock (10)
Wallop Primary School

TORNADOES

Tornadoes go round and round
They pick you up and
Throw you down.
They suck up cars
And lorries.
Whoops it
Sucked
Me up
A
a
a
a
a
a
h
h
h
h
!

Dean Stevenson (9)
Wallop Primary School

SAMMY SNAIL

Sammy Snail slithered slowly,
Straight down Slythering Street
And left silver trails
Sparkling in the sun.
Sammy Snail slid sleepily and went to sleep in his shell.
ZZZZZZZZZZ!

Nicola Marston (9)
Wallop Primary School

MORSE AND A HORSE

There once was a man called Morse
Who rode a happy man's horse
He smacked the horse's head
And certainly it was dead
Now, what a naughty man called Morse.

Now the naughty man was out of jail
His only job was to load up mail
Now the dead horse in Heaven
Can almost count up to seven
Now how I wonder why they let the man out of jail.

Emma Bennett (8)
Wallop Primary School

NONSENSE

One day I was walking down the street,
And what a peculiar animal I happened to meet.
Bright red lips with a fantastic smile,
That you could see from half a mile.
A brilliant hat sat upon its head,
With eyes as dark as pencil lead.
From all the weird things that it said,
The strangest things went through my head.
Then it said, 'I've really got to run,
I'm off to have a lot of fun.'
I hope I see that thing again,
Because it's still got my purple pen,
And that is why my poem must end.

Rebecca Warden-Brown (11)
Yateley Manor Preparatory School

THE MOON

When the sun goes down
The moon yawns and passes over the hill.
Then it rises
Up like a balloon.
The stars come out from hiding
And join the moon.
When the sun stretches
The stars scuttle away.
Then the moon goes to bed
And the sun takes over!

Adam Smith (11)
Yateley Manor Preparatory School

SPIDER

Spider, spider
Big and hairy
I think you
Are very scary.
When you're
In my bath
At night
Oh you
Give me
Such a fright.

Tom Baxter (10)
Yateley Manor Preparatory School

WHATEVER THE WEATHER

Whatever the weather
I don't care
As long as I breathe fresh air.

Spring and autumn
Come and go,
Will it rain?
Will it snow?

Blizzards frosts,
And ice to come.
Will we ever,
See the sun?

I like holidays
We have no school.
I like paddling
In my pool.

It's great when it is hot and sunny,
We go out with Dad and Mummy.
We go down the beach and sea
We all have fish and chips for tea.

Adam Dowthwaite (9)
Yateley Manor Preparatory School

THE ROOM

The room was nice but smaller than rice,
The room was smelly because there was a welly.
The room was wet because there was a pet.
The room was white it will give you a fright.
The room was cold because it was old.

Grant Murray (10)
Yateley Manor Preparatory School

MY BEST FRIEND

My best friend is called Jack,
He is a black and white cat.
He prowls around at night,
And usually gets into a fight.

When Jack comes home from a fight,
He is no longer black and white.
He is grey with bruises and scratches
And has lots of dark red patches.

When Jack comes through the cat-flap at night
My mother knows he's been in a fight
Quickly she bandages up his head,
Gives him some milk and sends him to bed.

Now you know Jack is my friend
I'm afraid that my poem must now
End.

Jade Dunham (10)
Yateley Manor Preparatory School

SNOW

The first flake falls, silently it settles,
Slowly a blanket forms,
Everything appears fresh and bright,
Until the children begin their snowball fight.
Snowmen appear and toboggans are ridden,
The children laugh and shout,
If we could have more fun-filled days,
Then we'd be champions on our sleighs!

Jamie O'Sullivan (10)
Yateley Manor Preparatory School

MANGO CHUTNEY

I like bacon, egg, sausage, mushrooms, all in red sauce.
Battered fish, battered sausage all with chips of course.
I like Mr Kiplings' yummy cakes they're all extremely nice.
Marshmallows, Munchies, Mars bars never fail to 'tice
But I'll tell you what I like the most
I'll tell you if you let me
It's the one all fruity taste of mango, mango chutney.

Hey mango, mango, mango, mango, mango,
Mango chutney!
Mango, mango, mango, mango, mango,
Mango chutney!

Harry Swinhoe & Jack Gardner (9)
Yateley Manor Preparatory School

THE BOY AND THE SPANIEL

The boy and the spaniel took to the air
In a beautiful big balloon.
They took some jam and a piece of ham
A knife, fork and a spoon.
The spaniel looked down to the clouds,
And howled at the ground below,
'Oh lovely ground, oh lovely ground,
What a long way away you are,
You are,
You are!
What a long way away you are.'

Neale Jones (10)
Yateley Manor Preparatory School

PLANETS

J   ust Jupiter has a red spot
U   p in swirling winds you'll find,
P   hoebe is a moon up high
I   o's close behind.
T   itan is the biggest
E   erie as it is,
R   ings swirl around it.

S   aturn has some fizz
A   ll the spinning rings around it
T   urning very fast,
U   nderneath are moons so bright
R   otating under cast.
N   ext there is the Earth.

E   veryone lives here,
A   nd it has its only moon
R   evolving as a sphere
T   ornadoes may appear around
H   urricanes may too.

And if you want to know about them
Then this poem is for you!

Charles Withall (9)
Yateley Manor Preparatory School

THE RABBIT AND THE HEDGEHOG

Starts fast, legs ache, carrot slice
Quick break! Eat much
Warm sun, hedgehog passed
Hedgehog's won!

Four feet, starts slow
Long way, food? No!
Keep on hedgehog's pace
Slowcoach
Wins race!

Peter Hodgson (10)
Yateley Manor Preparatory School

AN EARTHQUAKE IN INDIA

As we sit and wonder why
We can't have McDonalds for tea
Spare a thought for the boys and girls
From their homes and towns have had to flee.

Those who've been lying under rubble
Wondering if ever they'll be found
Causing rescuers insurmountable trouble
But continuing to search duty bound.

A two year old boy screams for his mother,
A father looking for his son,
A little girl finds her brother
Another day is done.

Every day things for granted we take
The earthquake has wiped away
The search dogs with teams all attempts make
To bring hope along the way.

I don't want McDonald's for tea
Can we go to the bank instead?
I'd like to donate one pound, two or three
To help keep the victims fed.

Oliver Howe (10)
Yateley Manor Preparatory School

THE ICE CREAM CONE RAP

'Yo Mum! I'm home. Can I have an ice cream cone?'

'Yeah sure, oops I dropped it on the floor.'

'Never mind I can get a different kind.'

'Is it cool or does it drool?'

'Ummm it's nice, I like it more than spice.'

'Here's another, for your brother.'

'So do you like it?'

'A little bit.'

Max Woolwich (10)
Yateley Manor Preparatory School

SACRIFICED

I lay on the stone table; it was incredibly cold,
This would be my last breath, as the story was told.
I had travelled far through forests, in my quest for gold,
Then I was captured by Aztec Indians, who were very bold.
The chieftain rose his knife aloft, making my blood run cold
I pleaded for mercy, my terror untold!
The knife came down, swishing and wishing
I prayed for forgiveness,
As I saw the gates of Heaven unfold.

James Riley (10)
Yateley Manor Preparatory School

ANTS

A is for ants, who eat all the crumbs.
B is for boys, who have trouble with sums.
C is for Carl, who catches wood lice.
D is for Daniel, who dodges the mice.
E is for Emma, who is my best friend.
F is for friendship, that will never end.

Hannah Williams (10)
Yateley Manor Preparatory School

A GERBIL'S LIFE

A gerbil's life is short
But sweet
Especially when it gets to eat
Tasty morsels every day
And sleep each night
On beds of hay.

Tim Smith (10)
Yateley Manor Preparatory School

CHOCOHOLIC

Are you a chocoholic or
Are you a toffeeholic or
Are you a sweetholic?

Well I am a sweetholic.
What are you?

Isaac Knight (9)
Yateley Manor Preparatory School

THE RAINBOW

The rainbow
It shows up like a flashing bow,
It makes a wonderful colour,
Nothing like any other!

If you find the end,
Your poorness it shall mend,
For you shall find something all bold,
Which is a big sack of gold!

There's red, orange, yellow and blue,
Indigo and violet just for you!
Those colours are they only ones,
But there's none like any buns!

Think of what the gold makes,
Think of all the cakes you can bake,
Think of the people that can't see the rainbows,
And think that you're very lucky!

Camilla Slater (10)
Yateley Manor Preparatory School

I FORGOT SOMETHING!

I was waiting for the bus
With my friend Hannah and Gus,
We waited for the bus to arrive
So that it could take us for a ride,
Myself and Hannah got on the bus
But guess what
We forgot Gus!

Sarah Easterbrook (10)
Yateley Manor Preparatory School

THE MONSTER UNDER MY BED

The monster is creepy,
The monster is scary,
The monster can hide
But the monster is not safe.

The monster is not fun,
The monster is not cool,
The monster is not good
But he is kind of cute.

The monster beats up my bro,
The monster went bad,
The monster hurt Mum
He beats me up!

Sarah Thomas (9)
Yateley Manor Preparatory School

DISEASE

I like my friends, they are kind and helpful
At break I ask them what we are playing
They normally say Bulldog or Disease
If I get hurt they take me to Matron.
Matron is kind-hearted and looks after me
I sit on her chair with an ice pack.
Me and my friends find the teacher on duty
I ask her to fill in a slip
Then we go back to our game of Disease
If someone catches it - can Matron stop it?

Morris Symington (9)
Yateley Manor Preparatory School

PETS

Feely hates Bolli so
She cries and spits wherever she goes
Bolli thinks it's fun to bark and nip
I think my Siamese cat will have a fit.

Louby Lou takes a different route
Loves to tease our little brute
Waiting for Bolli to run at her
She sits proudly still and doesn't stir.

Fat little Murphy joined this happy team
That affect made me want to scream
Barking at Bolli gave me a fright
But sleeping with the cats all through the night?

I wish my pets could just be friends
Then I wouldn't have to separate them
We could then just sit and play
And be happy that we live together every day!

Rosalind Allen (10)
Yateley Manor Preparatory School

RUGBY

Rugby is a muddy game
Without the mud it's not the same.
Muddy boys running around
In scrums and tackles they can be found.
Muddy knees and muddy faces
Mud is found in many places!

Patrick Crummay (9)
Yateley Manor Preparatory School

A WALK IN THE WOODS

Let's go!
The weather is fine
We can go out for a while.
It's boring being inside
It's much more fun
To play in the woods.

We run!
The grass is still wet
And the ground is muddy.
It's the middle of winter
It's cold and windy
We're having lots of fun.

We are tired!
The fresh air has been good.
We can walk home
Very slowly.
My boots feel heavy
From the mud.
My toes are cold,
My ears are red.

Mark Mellor (10)
Yateley Manor Preparatory School